Barack Hussein Obama's Presidency

This book presents research-based investigations of the communicative aspects of Barack Obama's presidency, with a focus on ethnicity, gender, and culture as they interact with communication. It examines Obama's rhetorical strengths, that also inform his visual rhetorical control, and looks beyond Obama's messaging to examine how the news framed his presidency.

The book opens by exploring the racio-rhetorical humor applied by President Obama during his presidency. Chapters investigate topics such as Obama's use of visual rhetoric, how the media framed Obama using racialized lens, and offer iconographical analysis of satires featured in *The New Yorker* that symbolized the politics of racial fear erupting prior to the start of Obama's presidency. They also examine how the White House used YouTube messaging to rebuild the first lady Michelle Obama's image in ways that became acceptable to a wider American public, Obama's rhetorical struggles to work within tensions created by the intersection of race and violence and analyze President Obama's speeches at Tribal Nations Conferences.

Barack Hussein Obama's Presidency will be a key resource for scholars and researchers of communication studies, political communication, media and cultural studies, race and ethnic studies, and political science, while also appealing to anyone interested in the communicative aspects of Obama's presidency and American politics. This book was originally published as a special issue of the *Howard Journal of Communications*.

Chuka Onwumechili is Professor of Communications at Howard University, USA and Editor-In-Chief of the *Howard Journal of Communications* (since 2015). He authored/co-edited more than 12 books and numerous academic articles. His most recent work is developing the African Cultural Theory of Communication (ACToC).

Barack Hussein Obama's Presidency
Rhetoric and Media Frames

Edited by
Chuka Onwumechili

NEW YORK AND LONDON

First published 2024
by Routledge
605 Third Avenue, New York NY 10158

and by Routledge
4 Park Square, Milton Park, Abingdon, Oxon, OX14 4RN

Routledge is an imprint of the Taylor & Francis Group, an informa business

© 2024 Taylor & Francis

All rights reserved. No part of this book may be reprinted or reproduced or utilised in any form or by any electronic, mechanical, or other means, now known or hereafter invented, including photocopying and recording, or in any information storage or retrieval system, without permission in writing from the publishers.

Trademark notice: Product or corporate names may be trademarks or registered trademarks, and are used only for identification and explanation without intent to infringe.

British Library Cataloguing in Publication Data
A catalogue record for this book is available from the British Library

ISBN13: 978-1-032-64068-6 (hbk)
ISBN13: 978-1-032-64069-3 (pbk)
ISBN13: 978-1-032-64070-9 (ebk)

DOI: 10.4324/9781032640709

Typeset in Minion Pro
by Newgen Publishing UK

Publisher's Note
The publisher accepts responsibility for any inconsistencies that may have arisen during the conversion of this book from journal articles to book chapters, namely the inclusion of journal terminology.

Disclaimer
Every effort has been made to contact copyright holders for their permission to reprint material in this book. The publishers would be grateful to hear from any copyright holder who is not here acknowledged and will undertake to rectify any errors or omissions in future editions of this book.

Contents

	Citation Information	vi
	Notes on Contributors	viii
	Introduction to Barack Hussein Obama's Presidency: Rhetoric and Media Frames Chuka Onwumechili	1
1	The Power of Obama's Racio-rhetorical Humor: Rethinking Black Masculinities Judy L. Isaksen	6
2	Image Control: The Visual Rhetoric of President Obama Timothy R. Gleason and Sara S. Hansen	20
3	"To Have Your Experience Denied … it Hurts": Barack Obama, James Baldwin, and the Politics of Black Anger Jeffrey B. Kurtz	37
4	News Framing of Obama, Racialized Scrutiny, and Symbolic Racism Srividya Ramasubramanian and Amanda R. Martinez	51
5	Technicolor Racism or Caricature Assassination? Satirizing White Anxiety About the Obama Presidency Elka M. Stevens and Tyson D. King-Meadows	70
6	State of Nations: Barack Obama's Indigenous America R. E. Glenn	91
7	Michelle Obama: Exploring the Narrative Marian Meyers and Carmen Goman	106
	Index	122

Citation Information

The chapters in this book were originally published in the *Howard Journal of Communications*, volume 28, issue 1 (2017). When citing this material, please use the original page numbering for each article, as follows:

Introduction

Introduction to the Special Issue on the Barack Hussein Obama Presidency
Chuka Onwumechili
Howard Journal of Communications, volume 28, issue 1 (2017), pp. 1–5

Chapter 1

The Power of Obama's Racio-rhetorical Humor: Rethinking Black Masculinities
Judy L. Isaksen
Howard Journal of Communications, volume 28, issue 1 (2017), pp. 6–19

Chapter 2

Image Control: The Visual Rhetoric of President Obama
Timothy R. Gleason and Sara S. Hansen
Howard Journal of Communications, volume 28, issue 1 (2017), pp. 55–71

Chapter 3

"To Have Your Experience Denied . . . it Hurts": Barack Obama, James Baldwin, and the Politics of Black Anger
Jeffrey B. Kurtz
Howard Journal of Communications, volume 28, issue 1 (2017), pp. 93–106

Chapter 4

News Framing of Obama, Racialized Scrutiny, and Symbolic Racism
Srividya Ramasubramanian and Amanda R. Martinez
Howard Journal of Communications, volume 28, issue 1 (2017), pp. 36–54

Chapter 5

Technicolor Racism or Caricature Assassination? Satirizing White Anxiety About the Obama Presidency
Elka M. Stevens and Tyson D. King-Meadows
Howard Journal of Communications, volume 28, issue 1 (2017), pp. 72–92

Chapter 6
State of Nations: Barack Obama's Indigenous America
R. E. Glenn
Howard Journal of Communications, volume 28, issue 1 (2017), pp. 107–121

Chapter 7
Michelle Obama: Exploring the Narrative
Marian Meyers and Carmen Goman
Howard Journal of Communications, volume 28, issue 1 (2017), pp. 20–35

For any permission-related enquiries please visit:
www.tandfonline.com/page/help/permissions

Notes on Contributors

Timothy R. Gleason, College of Letters and Science, Journalism, University of Wisconsin Oshkosh, Oshkosh, Wisconsin, USA.

R. E. Glenn, Department of Communication, Tulsa Community College, Tulsa, Oklahoma, USA.

Carmen Goman, Department of Communication Georgia State University, Atlanta, Georgia, USA.

Sara S. Hansen, College of Letters and Science, Journalism, University of Wisconsin Oshkosh, Oshkosh, Wisconsin, USA.

Judy L. Isaksen, Nido R. Qubein School of Communication, High Point University, High Point, North Carolina, USA.

Tyson D. King-Meadows, College of Liberal Arts, University of Massachusetts Boston, Boston, USA.

Jeffrey B. Kurtz, Department of Communication, Denison University, Granville, Ohio, USA.

Amanda R. Martinez, Department of Communication Studies, Davidson College, Davidson, North Carolina, USA.

Marian Meyers, Department of Communication Georgia State University, Atlanta, Georgia, USA.

Chuka Onwumechili, Department of Communication Studies, Howard University, Washington D.C., USA.

Srividya Ramasubramanian, S.I. Newhouse School of Public Communications, Syracuse University, USA.

Elka M. Stevens, Department of Art, Howard University, Washington, DC, USA.

Introduction to Barack Hussein Obama's Presidency: Rhetoric and Media Frames

On November 4, 2008, Barack Hussein Obama was elected America's 44th president and sworn in the next January 20. He was re-elected in 2012 and his 8 years in office ended January 20, 2017. It was a historic presidential tenure for various reasons. His wife, Michelle, summed her husband's tenure in the White House best when she spoke these words at the 2016 Democratic Party convention: "I wake up every morning in a house that was built by slaves. And I watch my daughters, two beautiful, intelligent black young women, playing with their dogs on the White House lawn." Those words spoke volumes by highlighting the monumental fact that a Black man, Barack Obama, served as America's president, which marked a long journey of Blacks in America from slavery. As several of the articles in this special issue confirm, Obama's tenure is historic for other reasons as well.

History will show that there remains a long way to go in the journey of African Americans in America. In fact, the 8-year presidential tenure of President Barack Obama reminds all of us there are challenges that are yet to be overcome. Foremost among them is that racial issues largely remain and there is the feeling that President Obama may not have done enough on Black issues.

Of course, it is not surprising that some of President Obama's achievements will be vigorously contested. However, his achievements will stand the test of time. Waldman (2016) concurs by writing,

> I wrote (before the 2008 elections) that he (Obama) had four great tasks before him. "If he sees the country through the current economic crisis, brings the war in Iraq to an end, passes health-care reform … and sets the country on a course away from reliance on fossil fuels, Obama would be considered the most important president since Franklin D. Roosevelt." To varying degrees he has done all four. (para. 3 and 4)

Furthermore, Glastris, Cooper, and Hu (2012) counted among President Obama's successes the passing of health care reform after five previous presidents had failed in attempts to pass similar reforms. Obama passed an almost $800 billion stimulus that reduced unemployment claims after a recession that was regarded as the biggest since the Great Depression of the 1920s. Also, he passed the Wall Street Reform that would push back on lending excesses of financial houses. However, there were also failures, including concerns about his handling of relations with Iran and his failure to resolve the intractable Iraq war. There were also claims of racial timidity (Coates, 2012; Dyson, 2016; West, 2014).

The *Howard Journal of Communications*, in keeping with its focus on "ethnicity, gender, and culture as they interact with communication," examines how Obama's Presidency is viewed from the lens of his and other's communications. There is a great deal of writing in this area, ranging from the novelty of his presidential campaign's extensive use of online social networking and his presidency's public engagement using social media (Adams & McCorkindale, 2013; Boys, 2010; Cogburn & Espinoza-Vasquez, 2011) to the inevitable analyses of Obama's encounters with racial discourses (Cisneros, 2015; Joseph, 2011; McKittrick, 2012).

Racial discourse was, particularly, pervasive during President Obama's tenure. A major marker of this discourse was Obama's relationship with controversial preacher Jeremiah Wright (Frank, 2009). Though the controversy occurred before Obama's 2008 election, the discourse was loaded with racial innuendos and throughout his presidency those innuendos were never fully erased as they always lurked in the background and sometimes appeared in the foreground. Further, President Obama's dogged attempt to maintain or occupy the space of postracial discourse was always tenuous and questioned. Sweet and McCue-Enser (2011) described President Obama's oratorical positioning on this issue as one in which Obama constructed his audience, the people, as constantly in flux, always being perfected but never fully finished, yet available to negotiate a national identity in the process of seeking a "perfect" nation.

Beyond the gaze at Obama, there is always an imagination of the inner feelings of the dominant racial group. After all, they had trusted Obama and saw in him as one that they could negotiate with in a vision of a new America. Brown (2011) interviewed 16 White men, who were in leadership positions in various organizations across America, to explore what these males imagined. In the end, Brown learned that members of the dominant racial group may rework racial ideologies when desired by reading racial meanings onto the actions of a popular Black leader. These meanings were in flux, dynamic, and indeterminate as opinion polls demonstrated throughout President Obama's tenure.

Contents of this special issue

President Obama's tenure, ultimately, was about disparate issues, but we narrow our focus on ethnicity, gender, and culture as they interact with communication. Therefore, this special issue seeks to capture meanings of President Obama's communications and other's communications about him. The articles published here are those selected from blind reviews following a call for papers distributed more than a year before the end of Barack Obama's presidency. They represent some of the strongest articles on Obama's presidency to date.

The first article by Judy L. Isaksen explores President Obama's use of humor and comedy in messaging. The article argues his use of humor and comedy is intentional and represents a way of negotiating Black masculinity. Isaksen argues that the social perceptions of Black masculinity view Black males as "violent and threatening," among other pathologies, and require means of identity negotiation and dismantling of pre-existing perceptions. For President Obama, the use of humor and comedy becomes a means of overcoming those pre-existing perceptions. Isaksen provides examples of Obama's use of humor, including his use of humor to confront questions about his religion and nationality. Isaksen argues Obama's intentional use of humor allows him to critique the dominant culture's construction of intersectional identities of race, gender, religion and citizenry.

Yet, Obama's presidency was not always about President Obama. In many ways, his wife, First Lady Michelle Obama, was frequently the focus of discourse among Americans. Thus, Marian Meyers and Carmen Goman's article exploring narratives on Michelle Obama is quite appropriate. Meyers examines YouTube videos designed to redefine the First Lady, following earlier media framing of her as an unpatriotic and angry Black woman. Meyers' study deviates from her previous work (2013) and Mortensen (2015) that examined online representation of the First Lady. The current article explores meanings within narratives provided by the White House and the first lady via YouTube videos. Meyers' article discovers two primary themes: (a) education, hard work, and perseverance which are narrated as important for success; and (b) motherhood and family. The two, she argues, denote achievement of the American Dream.

The third article by Srividya Ramasubramanian and Amanda R. Martinez uses experimental design to investigate news framing of President Obama. The article specifically examines whether exposure to negatively framed stories (compared to positively framed stories) on President Obama result in symbolic racist beliefs that are mediated by an anti-Black effect and increased stereotypical perceptions of African Americans. The results of the path analysis confirm that negatively framed stories lead to symbolic racism from anti-Black affect. However, the study notes that the type of story—positively or negatively framed—did not impact stereotypical perceptions. The author believes that the nonsignificant finding regarding stereotypical perceptions could be explained by current social tendencies among White Americans not to publicly admit stereotypical perceptions of a racial group.

Timothy R. Gleason and Sara S. Hansen's article analyzes official photographs from the White House by examining image control, visual rhetoric of images, and possible motivations of the presidential office in controlling images of the president. Hansen argues that the study is important because of the Presidency's decision to stop photojournalists from photographing certain White House events in 2013. Hansen uses Althusser's (2014) ideological state apparatus and visual rhetoric to examine ten images photographed without photojournalists. She finds the images attempt to connect the president with past leaders (with their images as background) and power. Hansen, however, notes the images often project President Obama's uneasiness in a suit compared to his images during informal settings. Hansen attempts to explain the Presidency's attempt to control photographed images by citing the White House staff's discomfort with Fox News' adversarial reports on Obama's tenure.

Prior to the 2008 presidential election, *The New Yorker* magazine featured on its front cover a caricature of Barack and Michelle Obama that raised the specter of racism and religious identity. Elka M. Stevens and Tyson D. King-Meadows' article, "Technicolor Racism or Caricature Assassination? Satirizing White Anxiety About the Obama Presidency," interrogates the defense of the image as satire and also uses secondary analysis of survey data from a Pew study to examine support for caricature. Stevens' iconographical analysis concludes the caricature depicted the Obamas as connected to each other but disconnected from American values. These conclusions follow deep analysis of dress, body, and background of the images. The data analysis suggests that although Republicans and Whites endorsed the image as a caricature and funny, Democrats and non-Whites saw the images as offensive and racist.

Jeffrey B. Kurtz's article focuses on President Obama's rhetorical struggles to work within tensions created by the intersection of race and violence. Kurtz examines four cases involving Obama's spoken responses to shootings in Tucson, Newtown, and Charleston and then the not-guilty verdict of George Zimmerman for the murder of Trayvon Martin. Kurtz's argues that Obama inherits James Baldwin's civic anger in challenging citizens to seek reconciliation during difficult moments. Obama's decision to construct this line of rhetoric earned him critics but Kurtz argues it invites us to deeply rethink how we approach tense racial situations, particularly embedded in politically and racially charged lynchings. Kurtz labels this as productive civic anger.

Finally, R. E. Glenn's essay is an analysis of President Obama's speeches at Tribal Nations Conferences. Glenn argues that President Obama's relationship with indigenous Americans is unique in American presidential history. Glenn's essay notes that demands of indigenous Americans differ significantly from those of minorities. He argues that although minorities agitate for participation in the American Dream, indigenous Americans seek to be separated from it and to return to precolonial systems. He then argues an examination of President Obama's speeches at the annual Tribal Nations Conferences presents America not as a unity of states but rather as a state of differing nations. Glenn concludes that President Obama has been friendly to indigenous nations and has advanced some of their needs by establishing the Indian Healthcare Improvement Act as part of the Affordable Care Act and implementing programs to improve access to broadband Internet for indigenous communities.

Conclusion

This special issue on Barack Obama's presidency is intended to record exemplars of President Obama's communication during his historic tenure as the 44th president of the United States. It was a remarkable tenure that included many activities and achievements that were important to communication scholarship, particularly in the area of culture, ethnicity, and communication. Although we do not claim that articles in this special issue are exhaustive, we certainly present them as representative of President Obama's time in office. As Waldman (2016) has claimed, it was and continues to be a presidential tenure not only remarkable for its racially historic footnote but a tenure where "Obama would be considered the most important president since Franklin D. Roosevelt" (para. 4).

Chuka Onwumechili

References

Adams, A., & McCorkindale, T. (2013). Dialogue and transparency: A content analysis of how the 2012 presidential candidates used twitter. *Public Relations Review, 39*, 357–359.

Althusser, L. (2014). *On the reproduction of capitalism: Ideology and ideological state apparatuses.* New York, NY: Verso Books.

Boys, S. (2010). The millennials refuse to be ignored! An analysis of how the Obama administration furthers the political engagement of a new generation. *The International Journal of Public Participation, 4*, 31–42.

Brown, C. (2011). Barack Obama as the 'Great Man': Communicative constructions of racial transcendence in white male elite discourses. *Communication Monographs, 78*, 535–556.

Cisneros, J. (2015). A nation of immigrants and a nation of laws: Race, multiculturalism, and neoliberal exception in Barack Obama's immigration discourse. *Communication, Culture & Critique, 8*, 356–375.

Coates, T. (2012, September). Fear of a black president. *The Atlantic.* Retrieved from http://www.theatlantic.com/magazine/archive/2012/09/fear-of-a-black-president/309064/

Cogburn, D., & Espinoza-Vasquez, F. (2011). From networked nominee to networked nation: Examining the impact of web 2.0 and social media on political participation and civic engagement in the 2008 Obama campaign. *Journal of Political Marketing, 10*, 189–213.

Dyson, M. (2016). *The black presidency: Barack Obama and the politics of race in America.* Boston, MA: Houghton Mifflin Harcourt.

Frank, D. (2009). The prophetic voice and the face of the Other in Barack Obama's "A more perfect union" address, March 18, 2008. *Rhetoric & Public Affairs, 12*, 167–194.

Glastris, P., Cooper, R., & Hu, S. (2012, March/April). Obama's Top 50 accomplishments. *The Washington Monthly.* Retrieved from http://washingtonmonthly.com/magazine/marchapril-2012/obamas-top-50-accomplishments/

Joseph, R. (2011). Imagining Obama: Reading overtly and inferentially racist images of our 44th President, 2007–2008. *Communication Studies, 62*, 389–405.

McKittrick, K. (2012). Quiescent change: Reading Barack Obama, reading race and racism, reading Whiteness. *Qualitative Sociology, 35*, 243–249.

Meyers, M. (2013). *African American women in the news: Gender, race, and class in journalism.* New York, NY: Routledge.

Mortensen, T. (2015). Visually assessing the First Lady in a digital age: A study of Michelle Obama as portrayed by journalists and the White House. *Journal of Women, Politics, and Policy, 36*, 43–67.

Sweet, D., & McCue-Enser, M. (2011). Constituting 'The People' as rhetorical interruption: Barack Obama and the unfinished hopes of an imperfect people. *Communication Studies, 62*(1), 602–622.

Waldman, P. (2016, January 6). The extraordinarily complicated successes of President Obama. *TheWeek.* Retrieved from http://theweek.com/articles/597635/extraordinarily-complicated-successes-president-obama

West, C. (2014). *Black prophetic fire.* Boston, MA: Beacon Press.

The Power of Obama's Racio-rhetorical Humor: Rethinking Black Masculinities

Judy L. Isaksen

ABSTRACT
This article examines Obama's savvy use of humor and argues that his intentional comedic communication offers a new model of negotiating Black masculinity. The author grounds her argument by discussing the contradictions, oppressive cultural perceptions, and instabilities of gender and racial repertoires that challenge the existence of all Black men, including our president. To disrupt these challenges, she posits that Obama engages in intentional performative practices of comedy to attain and sustain his own sense of Black masculinity. Next she unpacks Obama's comedic style, further positing that the true value of his comedy lies in the purpose and effect of his rhetorical messaging. To support her theorizing, she then analyzes a variety of comedic experiences in which Obama's humorous intentionality provides an emancipatory, rearticulated paradigm for rethinking Black masculinities. Finally, the author demonstrates the ways in which Obama's racio-rhetorical style, via humor, is already influencing other Black men.

Our 44th president, Barack Obama, is often characterized by his calm, laid-back demeanor, but he is also a man of impassioned feelings who has been unabashedly demonstrative with his emotions throughout his presidency. We have delighted in watching his loving interactions with his wife and daughters; we have witnessed him joyfully honor Al Green as well as mournfully honor Reverend Pinckney with song; we have heard his voice choke up with emotion and watched him wipe away tears; we have seen him interact with kids with a childlike exuberance and embrace prisoners with a brotherly empathy. And still yet another vitally important aspect of his impassioned personality exists—namely, his deadpan and deeply self-referential sense of humor.

Obama is a man who repeatedly and confidently demonstrates his propensity for mirth and amusement; in an interview with comedian Marc Maron, Obama (2015b) counted Richard Pryor, Jerry Seinfeld, and Louis C.K. among his favorites, indicating a life-long love of comedy, a love that clearly didn't get tabled once he became president. In fact, our president's playful side stands as one of his hallmark characteristics. After all, he is the first sitting president to make a late night TV appearance, going on *The Tonight Show With Jay Leno* in 2013 (Lichter, Baumgartner, & Morris, 2015) and has been a regular—and quite funny—guest on *The Colbert Report*, *The Tonight Show Starring Jimmy Fallon*, and *The Daily Show*, where he visited with Jon Stewart seven times. Equally telling is the opinion that professional comedians have of Obama's comedic chops. Seth Meyers (2011), for example, chatting with Letterman, lamented that razzing the president is a problem because "he's really funny." Likewise, Jerry Seinfeld (2015) invited Obama to join him on his web series *Comedians in Cars Getting Coffee*, stating Obama "has gotten off just enough funny lines to qualify," and note that the caliber of Seinfeld's other guests include such luminaries as Mel Brooks, Tina Fey, Steve Martin, Will Ferrell, and Julia Louis-Dreyfus. Dean Obeidallah (2016) of *The Atlantic* called Obama the "killer comedian in chief," stating that "No U.S. President has been a better comedian than Barack Obama. It's really that simple." Beyond his material, Obeidallah is impressed with Obama's comedic delivery, and when he had the opportunity to personally compliment the president on his timing, he writes that Obama "paused just long enough, and then responded: 'I know.'" When Obama is in his comedic groove, his self-referential awareness bespeaks a coolness that says, "Yes, I'm the president, and yes, I am damn funny."

As the president who has undoubtedly enjoyed a more mediated and comedic presence than any preceding president, investigating the consequences of his rhetorical use of comedy—through the lenses of race and gender—is a fruitful endeavor. I contend that with his savvy use of humor, Obama, notwithstanding 8 years of managing difficult national and international affairs, leaves his presidency with a special legacy that reaches far beyond his policies—namely, a new model of negotiating Black masculinity.

My argument unfolds in three parts: first, I ground my argument by discussing the contradictions, oppressive cultural perceptions, and instabilities of gender and racial repertoires that challenge the existence of all Black men, including our president. To disrupt these challenges, I posit that Obama engages in intentional performative practices of comedy to attain and sustain his own sense of Black masculinity. Next I unpack Obama's comedic style, further positing that the true value of his comedy is not the laughter he evokes, although he is quite funny, but rather the purpose and effect of his rhetorical messaging. Lastly, I support my suggested theorizing by analyzing a variety of comedic experiences—and my sample is limited to his discourse that deals with sites of identity, primarily with matters of race and gender—in which Obama's comedic intentionality provides an emancipatory model for rethinking Black masculinities. All joking aside, I posit that Obama's use of rhetorical comedy simultaneously achieves three ends: he challenges, disrupts, and discards the perceptions imposed on Black men by society; he models a discursive means that is confident, intelligent, and effective; and he opens up a space for Black men to follow suit, which is, in fact, already publically occurring.

The challenges that complicate Black American masculinities

When Barack Obama entered the presidency in 2008, he brought with him a rich collection of multiplicities and experiences that straddles races, continents, cultures, and classes, all of which construct his identity as a man, more specifically as a Black man. Cultural studies theorists Shaw and Watson (2011) in their exploration of Obama's masculinities cogently argue that these multiplicities are the "essential contradictions" (p. 134) that root and ground Obama. Moreover, Shaw and Watson point out that Obama himself is fully aware that masculinity, as a site of identity, is an ever-shifting construction. In fact, long before scholars and cultural critics began exploring our president's masculinity, Obama had already been publically analyzing himself. Both of his books, *Dreams From My Father* (1995) and *The Audacity of Hope* (2006) are populated with anecdotes in which Obama regularly analyzes himself, letting "us know that he is aware of the clash of masculinities in his whole self—the contradictory gap between the ideal and the real" (Shaw & Watson, 2011, p. 147).

This gap between the cultural perceptions of hegemonic masculinity, which is highly contingent and socially constructed (Connell, 1995; Johnson, 1997; Kimmell, 2011), vis à vis the material reality of Black men is at the root of theorizing about Black masculinities. The repertoires of both gender and race are inherently contradictory and unstable, which keeps us all in a constant state of negotiation; for Black men that state of negotiation is even more agitating. "While race may have the appearance of reflecting an 'inner essence,' this is a phantasy." Race, racial categories, and racial norms are continually produced and reproduced; further, we are "born into these norms and our subjectivity is fashioned in, by and through them" (Ehlers, 2012, p. 70). Coupled with the oppression that Black men are born into, an array of disciplinary practices within cultural institutions—media, law, education—further contribute to our societal imprinting of such perceptions of Black masculinity. Jackson (2006), for example, in his exploration of the Black masculine corporeal body being read as a communicative, discursive text, argues cogently that the Black male body is often "viewed as a threat" (p. 99), specifically that Black male bodies, and therefore Black male lives are regularly pathologized and labeled variously as innately exotic, violent, sexual, exploitable, and irresponsible (p. 75). These scripted "identities are deployed and negotiated with struggle at the center of the exchange" (p. 100), struggles that stem from attributed identities from "inscribed social predicates" (p. 100). Positioning the Black body as threatening, in turn, creates a society that deems it acceptable to casually devalue, imprison, even kill Black men, and so the cycle continues. This problematic cycle necessitates Black males, including our president, to work intentionally to disrupt such erroneous perceptions and norms to have a shot at *earning* their masculinity, something that should be an inalienable right.

Obama's rhetorical intentionality diligently attempts to dismantle the pre-existing cultural identity norms that set up an uncomfortable tension between his own self-identity against the attributed identity that is thrust upon him by others, based solely on the fact that he is a "member of a particular identity group"—namely, a Black male. As a result, Obama is forced to relentlessly negotiate his identity within Black masculinity and manage the tension by adopting particular "performance practices" and particular "signaling behaviors" to consistently communicate his own identity with accuracy (Cooper, 2003, pp. 842–846). Each time Obama engages in these signaling practices, his performativity—in both the racial and gender modalities—is creating counterhegemonic reworkings and rearticulations of Black masculinity. Each time Obama engages in these signaling practices, his performativity is rhetorically modeling, for all Black men, an emancipatory means to not only attain but to also delight in one's own authentic self-identity.

Obama's humor and his rhetorical effect

We know, theoretically and materially, that masculinities and the performativity of Black masculinity is difficult to navigate, loaded with inherent social constructs that, too often, unwittingly make men complicit in the creation of their own hardships. Negotiating this terrain, successfully, demands not only constant attention but also new tools and sensibilities, and humor is certainly a useful one.

The humor experience as a form of communication plays out in a most significant way: It brings about change, whether in our perceptions, cognitions, or physiological responses; we are altered, aroused, loosened, possibly transformed. Waisanen (2015), in his analysis of the presidential use of the enthymematic style of comedy to rhetorically manage crises, cogently proves that jokes by "those *in* power" (p. 336) are an effective tool for managing perceptions as humor bids both the rhetor and the audience "to participate in the construction of meaning" (p. 339). Indeed, the rhetorical effect of any humorous experience, in terms of meaning-making, can be plotted along a continuum with a unifying or divisive reaction on the polar ends. As a unifier, humor wins affection, affirms mutual care, maintains consensus, and narrows social distances in groups; conversely, when humor operates divisively it can enact conflict, reiterate antagonisms, alienate outsiders, and reinforce social boundaries. In the effects-based humor typology created by communication scholar Meyer (2000, 2015), he includes, along a continuum from unifying to dividing, four key functions of humor: identification and clarification on the unifying end, and enforcement and differentiation on the dividing end of the continuum. A close look at Obama's use of humor indicates that, save for the extreme end of the divisive differentiation, he travels quite a distance along Meyer's continuum.

In fact, Obama most enjoys the dialogic tension of melding together humor that both unifies and divides; such humor roughens up the mutual care yet doesn't fully alienate, it builds from points of conflict while also winning affection. Fully embodying his "essential contradictions," Obama casually tosses a high-energy and incisive barb, but he successfully delivers it with an innocent schoolboy smile. This type of humor is often associated with what humor theorists (McGhee, 1979; Meyer, 2000, 2015; Morreall, 1983) generally refer to as superiority humor—that is, laughter experienced as enjoyment over another's flaws, misfortune, or improper behavior.

Obama also makes great use of incongruity humor, which relies purely on the surprising jolt; when we encounter an idea that is unexpected, we experience laughter. And although Obama sprinkles in the occasional self-deprecating humor that falls on the extreme end of unifying continuum—and notably the comedic style most of his predecessors typically used—he clearly favors a more edgy comedy style, one that has social purpose. Humor theorists agree that self-deprecatory comedy is designed to eliminate all sense of superiority and enhance a shared sense of humanity, aspects we expect Obama to value; however, when it comes to matters of Black masculinity, Obama has richer rhetorical goals. He doesn't waste too many comedic moments on his graying hair or other prevailing narratives of hegemonic masculinity. Rather than feeding into existing power structures, he intentionally uses comedy to disrupt the predicated cultural norms that have been stifling Black men for centuries. Obama's style of comedy in delivery, intensity, and rhetorical messaging, like those of our best sociopolitical comedians—Jon Stewart, Samantha Bee, John Oliver, Stephen Colbert, Larry Wilmore, and Key and Peele—is rhetorically sophisticated and purposeful.

Taking full advantage of his position of power, Obama's use of humor is not merely constructing meaning—he is *re*constructing meaning. He is the only president to make matters of race, ethnicity, gender, and religion the subjects of humor. No other president has personally joked about these matters, though each man has indeed been gendered and raced. By boldly addressing matters of identity in comedic communication, he is enacting a different way of performing Black masculinity, while simultaneously calling into question the challenges that Black men face. Throughout Obama's presidency we are witnessing a fresh new paradigm and re-articulation of Black masculinity that puts at its center not threats and struggles, but confidence and boldness. What follows is an analysis of Obama's use of humor and the rhetorical effects he creates for not only his purpose at hand but also as a fresh, authentic, and effective model of Black masculinity.

Have you heard the one about the Kenyan Muslim? Through the comic lens of enforcement

Obama is continually forced to contend with a manufactured and ritualized discourse of ideological fears that position him as a threatening outsider, despite the fact that he is the president of the United States. This construction began even before he was first elected, as exemplified by the July 2008 *New Yorker* cover appropriately entitled "The Politics of Fear." The cover art depicts hyperbolic caricatures of Barack in Muslim garb and Michelle in Black Nationalist garb unified by their fist-bumping in the Oval Office. This brilliant satire, including the hanging portrait of bin Laden and the burning American flag, targets the distortions and misconceptions that the Obamas were facing on the campaign trail concerning their patriotism, citizenship, and religion. After his election, the discourse of fear and antagonism continued to haunt him with Donald Trump and his followers leading the way. The latest poll of CNN (2015) on Obama's religion and citizenship—a poll for 7 years running—indicates that the fear is unrelenting. Thirty percent of all Republicans and 39% of Trump supporters still believe that Obama was not born in America; similarly, 43% of Republicans and 54% of Trump supporters believe Obama is Muslim. It is notable that Obama's opponents and CNN's repeated polling address only Obama's religion and nationality and fully gloss over any mention of race; in doing so, they are adhering to the our cultural narrative of colorblindness, which erases all matters of race so as not to face our historic institutional racism or our responsibility to it. Obama's opponents are presumably driven by racial fear, but such fears must be rhetorically expressed through subterfuge, so they turn to the ostensibly safer targets of religion and citizenry. Rossing (2011) found this same deracialization—papering over of racial matters—at work back in 2008 regarding the *New Yorker* cover. With the exception of a few progressive media outlets and perspectives written by people of color, the prolific discourses within mainstream media entirely elided matters of race in "The Politics of Fear," choosing instead to individually scapegoat the magazine's editors, thereby failing to see, and thus challenge, our culture's deeply entrenched systemic racism.

These ongoing insults attack the very core of Obama's identity and illustrate the hurdles he, and others, face as Black men in America. Yet Obama responds to these constructions not by the expected racialized and gendered scripted performances of anger, nor with cool detachment (Majors & Billson, 1992); rather, Obama boldly responds with the emancipatory performance practices of humor. He takes these unwanted attributed identities—of being Muslim and born in Kenya—and rhetorically turns them back on his oppressors. With each biting delivery addressing these trifling matters, Obama is engaging in what Meyer terms an enforcement type of humor. Note that this type is toward the divisive end of the humor continuum. Obama is calmly but unabashedly performing his self-identity through humor, but humor with an aggressive edge. Enforcement humor, according to Meyer (2015), claims that we all get the joke, but I'm laughing at your expense, and you know it. Obama is violated by this continual discrediting, but just as relentlessly he, via humor, reminds his haters that they are being disciplined through laughter.

News reports indicate that Obama delivers these birth- and religion-based jokes where and whenever he can—on the campaign trail, at State Dinners, in Kenya, on late night TV—but assuredly at the long-standing tradition of the White House Correspondents Dinner (WHCD), the annual gathering of journalists, politicos, and celebrities. This Washington event, which is typically hosted by a comedian and provides an opportunity for presidential humor, is where Obama most prominently displays his comedic chops. At the 2015 WHCD, tucked into this list of overwhelming obligations, Obama (2015a), with a deadpan facial expression, not only reiterates who holds the power but also casually drops a searing jab at those who disrespectfully deny him his own identity as a Christian man in America: "Anyway, being president is never easy. I still have to fix a broken immigration system, issue veto threats, negotiate with Iran, all while finding time to pray five times a day." Moments later he again skewers his doubters when he refers to Jeb's misstep of calling himself Hispanic back in 2009; Obama calls Bush's gaffe an "innocent mistake"—"reminds me of when I identified myself as American back in (pause) 1961." However, Obama's most powerful comedic disruption of the endless badgering by Trump and the "birther movement" comes at his 2011 WHCD opening remarks; with mock-serious facial expressions and his slow and measured cadence, he, through both superiority and enforcement, gets the last laugh:

> My fellow Americans. (Laughter and applause.) Mahalo! (Laughter.) It is wonderful to be here at the White House Correspondents Dinner. What a week. (Laughter.) As some of you heard, the state of Hawaii released my official long-form birth certificate. (Applause.) Hopefully this puts all doubts to rest. But just in case there are any lingering questions, tonight I'm prepared to go a step further. (Laughter.) Tonight, for the first time, I am releasing my official birth video. (Laughter.) Now, I warn you—(Laughter)—no one has seen this footage in 50 years, not even me. But let's take a look.

The 20-second clip, playfully time-stamped 04 Aug 1961 PM 7:24, is the definitive scene from Disney's *The Lion King* when baby Simba, the symbol of power, is grandly unveiled and all in the African kingdom bow down to him in praise, notably a scene reminiscent of *Roots* when newborn Kunta Kinte is held skyward by his father. This clowning on Trump, who is in the audience and the camera pans to twice, is laced with Obama's moxie as he refuses the construction that Trump and his haters place upon him, flips the script and points out who truly holds the power, all while using their point of irritation—their fear of Africa—to do so.

Further, Obama (2011) topped his joke with a meta-joke, deriding Fox News's inability to discern truth from fiction:

> I want to make clear to the Fox News table: That was a joke. (Laughter.) That was not my real birth video. (Laughter.) That was a children's cartoon. (Laughter.) Call Disney if you don't believe me. (Laughter.) They have the original long-form version. (Laughter.)

And he refuses to let up. Eight years after this demeaning construction began, Obama (2016), at his final WHCD, still takes disciplinary jabs at his adversaries about his outsider status: "Ted [Cruz] had a tough week. He went to Indiana, Hoosier country"—and here Obama flashes a smirk—"stood on a basketball court," and with a completely straight face, finishes his line which he delivers slowly and emphatically "and called the hoop a basketball ring." Obama continues to joke about Cruz's lack of sports familiarity, but the biggest laughs and applause come when he subtly drops his self-referential capper: "Hah, but sure, I'm the foreign one." It appears that Obama will not pass up an opportunity to call out his trollers and declare his own identity to the world.

Through enforcement of his own sense of male identity, Obama, in his sometimes subtle, sometimes bold use of humor, continually engages in signaling behaviors to those who disregard him as a leader, signaling behaviors that only embolden his identity as a strong, bold, and rhetorically witty Black man.

A new version of masculinity goes viral: Through the lenses of identification and clarification

Although Obama effectively uses humor to deflect bigotry, he also brilliantly uses it for matters of persuasion, engaging in what Meyer (2000, 2015) theorized as identification and clarification on the unifying end of the continuum. Meyer noted that humor through identification is built on a shared value system between speaker and audience, where everyone gets the joke. Slightly more nuanced, humor of clarification functions to educate, persuade, or to correct misconceptions. With clarification humor, everyone gets the joke, but it suggests, "Let's take a second look, shall we?" President Obama has engaged in this type of playful, unifying humor on multiple occasions, such as Slow Jamming the New with Jimmy Fallon as well as taking over as host for The Word on *The Colbert Report*.

But a striking example of such playfulness that also simultaneously pushes back against the constructions of masculinity is Obama's appearance on Zach Galifianakis's irreverent web series *Between Two Ferns* (2014) to promote the Affordable Care Act. *Between Two Ferns* satirizes the lifeblood of celebrity culture—the interview—as Galifianakis and his guest sit awkwardly on a stark set between two ferns; typically guests play the irritated "straight man," enduring Galifianakis's nonsensical blather, but they can also improvise and dish it right back. And Obama does. With full consideration for the rhetorical situation—that he needed to reach young Americans; that they rely primarily on digital sources for content; that the deadline for signing up for health insurance was fast approaching; that the rollout of the program was riddled with problems—Obama boldly embraces comedy that is rooted in full-blown incongruity. And rhetorically, it worked; his segment identified with over 33 million viewers. Obama's performance of masculinity, however, did not go without pushback from conservatives who felt he demeaned the dignity of the office of the presidency. The outrage of "Fox and Friends" was only surpassed by the self-righteous and hyperbolic outrage of Colbert on *The Colbert Report*, which only added to the layers of hilarity and spurred more viewings.

Obama is hands-down funny, but the intentional subtext of this clip offers even more. Consider how the performance of each man pushes back against socially constructed masculinity for both Blacks and Whites. Galifianakis, this disheveled man-child, is the antithesis of an expected gendered script that includes a slim, well-groomed, well-articulated talk show host. Likewise, Obama isn't loud and ignorant; rather, he is suave, snarky, and entertaining, and he completely defies the pathologized representation of the threatening Black male. Neither man is performing gender according to our normalized disciplinary rules. If rhetorically, identification means building upon the shared value system between the speakers and their audience, then, most viewers would aspire to, or identify with, the version of masculinity comprised of the suave, intelligent, cool Black guy, and not the slobby, pasty, bumbling White guy.

Further, their improvised banter spoofs on problematic gender expectations when Obama razzes Galifianakis, claiming that Bradley Cooper "carried" the *Hangover* movies:

Galifianakis: Yeah, everybody loves Bradley. Good for him.
Obama: Good lookin' guy.
Galifianakis: Being like that in Hollywood, that's easy! Tall, handsome, that's easy. Be short, fat, and smell like Doritos and try to make it in Hollywood.

And when the discussion turns to Obama being president, a Black president, Obama, despite the comedic genre, readily envisions a future with Black leaders at the helm, and checks Galifianakis's logic with a final comic blow:

Galifianakis: I have to know. What is it like to be the last Black president?
Obama: Seriously? What's it like for this to be the last time you ever talk to a president?
Galifianakis: It must kinda stink though, that you can't run, you know, three times. You know?
Obama: No. Actually, I think it's a good idea. Uh, if I ran a third time, it'd be sorta like doing a third *Hangover* movie. It didn't really work out very well, did it?

As Obama skillfully provides the details for signing up for the Affordable Care Act, Galifianakis looks at his watch and mumbles insults, but Obama smoothly rolls with the punches and holds his own against the inanity. Refusing to oblige by the constraining cultural imperatives of not only the office of the presidency but also society's gendered and racial scripts, Obama playfully informs the populace while simultaneously critiquing the constraints of our gender repertoires. His rearticulated model of masculinity demonstrates that one can succeed at being silly and vulnerable, yet simultaneously snarky and powerful—namely, that humor is an effective tool for performing masculinity.

"Let me be clear": The fruition of Obama's racio-rhetorical style

We have seen the effective ways that Obama has modeled a fresh version of masculinity through humor while simultaneously critiquing the intersectional identities of religion, race, citizenry, and gender as constructed by the dominant culture. I now take a closer look at solely matters of race and the ways in which Obama's racio-rhetorical style—that is, the ways in which he is *reconstructing* matters of race through discourse—is effectively catching on with other Black men and filtering throughout society. For this, I layer onto Obama's humor the work of several professional Black comedians: host of *The Nightly Show* Larry Wilmore and sketch comedy team Key and Peele.

Wilmore (2015) has an ongoing segment on his show entitled "Obama Don't Care" that spoofs the president as he is "rolling out as much Black as he can his last year in office." Wilmore began the segment in response to the penultimate WHCD when we witnessed an admittedly "loose and relaxed" Obama (2015a) who brilliantly lambasted his recalcitrant Congress with his ornery Bucket List.

My advisors asked me "Mr. President, do you have a bucket list?" And I said, "Well, I have something that rhymes with bucket list."
Take executive action on immigration. Bucket.
New climate regulations. Bucket. It's the right thing to do.

Obama is toying with his performances of the expected and normative practices of hegemonic masculinity; he is not crossing the line of irreverence, but he is coming close enough to it that Wilmore sees the opportunity to build on Obama's freshness and comically carry it forward. Wilmore's "Obama Don't Care" segment features moments such as Michelle rapping to Chicago youth about education; Obama visiting Kenya and Obama publically dropping the n-word, acts he would have never done in his first term. As Obama nears the end of his presidency, he is repeatedly and boldly bringing Black culture to the forefront, and Wilmore is paying close attention and intentionally and comedically giving voice to Blackness.

Just a few moments after delivering his bucket list gag, Obama (2015a), in arguably his finest WHCD comedic moment, partners with another Black comedian as he brings on stage the character of Luther. Like Wilmore, the sketch comedy team Key and Peele have also been paying attention to Obama's refashioning of Black masculinity and, thus, introduced their recurring character based purely on Obama's racio-rhetoric—namely, "Luther, Obama's Anger Translator," performed brilliantly by Keegan-Michael Key. Precisely because Obama is so antithetical to the dominant constructions of Black masculinity—never showing anger, never raising his voice, never speaking the unspeakable—Key and Peele created Luther, a dude from the Southside of Chicago, whom Obama hires solely to express his unspoken rage. Key (2012), while visiting the *Conan* show, explains that Luther's origin was in response to the disrespectful audacity of House Representative Joe Wilson's interruption, calling Obama a liar as he was addressing Congress in 2009. Rather than Obama responding the way that society might expect based on the erroneous perceptions of Black masculinity, he calmly and quietly responds "not true." Key and Peele intentionally created Luther to give voice to and satirize the constructed norms of the angry Black man. In each of their many Luther skits, Jordan Peele, with uncanny precision, impersonates Obama as he calmly delivers his fireside chat, whereas Luther, in full animation and without a filter, bounces around the room verbally spouting Obama's inner indignations.

Obama (2012) openly shares with Jimmy Fallon that he not only enjoys Key and Peele's humor but he also appreciates and understands the rhetorical intent of their constructed Luther. In an unprecedented move, Obama daringly invites Luther to perform with him at the 2015 WHCD. Key (2015) admitted that at their rehearsal, Obama was finding it challenging to keep a straight face while Luther interjected his thoughts. At the event, however, Obama maintains his perfect deadpan delivery as Luther maniacally satirizes every stereotype that has plagued Black men throughout history while the audience is forced to imagine that these words are Obama's internal thoughts. Clearly, the comedic writing was intended to expose our culture's colorblind master narrative as Luther opens with a hyperbolical shout: "Hold on to your lily-white butts." Once again, addressing those who question Obama's faith and moral compass, Luther indicts Fox News for "terrifying old White people with some nonsense: Sharia law is coming to Cleveland. Run for the damn hills. Y'alls ridiculous." Likewise, Luther calls out CNN for 2 weeks of "wall-to-wall Ebola coverage," reifying problematic representations of Africa as the "Dark Continent" of disease and despair. But perhaps more powerful than the verbal communication is Luther's facial expressions and mannerisms, which speak volumes. He is loud, fuming, and manic; he is wide-eyed, stuttering, and stammering. He captures and is reminiscent of every debased and exaggerated image of Blacks in film, television, and cartoons that we have witnessed over the decades. Luther is putting these problematic representations in our faces, forcing us to confront our racist history. This bit is quite funny, but at the same time, Luther and our president are sending a compelling message as they are uncovering our racist past while simultaneously providing a bold new look at Black masculinity.

While his act with Luther stands as perhaps Obama's most audacious performance, the 2016 WHCD, Obama's last scheduled opportunity to use his comedic chops for social change, seems to take his messaging of Black masculinity to the next level—namely, when he, the front-runner, officially passes the baton onto his followers. Indeed, Obama drops a few race-related zingers, such as earning "some serious Tubmans" once he leaves the White House and questioning those who relentlessly wonder if he is "Black enough." And after sincerely thanking the press corps for their diligent work, he concludes his remarks unlike any other president has—"With that, I just have two more words to say: 'Obama out,'" which he immediately follows with a blown kiss and a mic drop. With two swift words and two swift motions, Obama's use of these cultural memes that intentionally signify bold confidence, is giving props to two culturally significant realms for Blacks and Black masculinity: basketball and hip hop. Be it Kobe or Kanye, with his closing, Obama is signifying a Black masculinity that is rooted in success, accomplishment, and pride. So, yes, we certainly get a solid dose of Obama's racio-rhetoric.

But I contend that it is the subtext of Obama's opening statements—his first two comments—that truly holds the message, indicating that his use of humor to model an emancipatory style of Black masculinity is indeed taking hold. Obama (2106) began with "It is an honor to be here at my last, and perhaps *the last* [emphasis added] White House Correspondents Dinner." As he says this, Obama pauses, physically turns his body, and smirks directly at Larry Wilmore, the evening's host comedian, whom we hear chuckling off camera. Although the audience laughs, these two men appear to share a knowing moment, prepared for what is about to come as Wilmore's remarks will follow the president's. It's important to note that Wilmore—an Emmy award-winning talent who wrote for *The Fresh Prince of Bel-Air* and *In Living Color*; was Jon Stewart's "Senior Black Correspondent;" is the executive producer of Black*ish*; and hosts of *The Nightly Show*—is a comedian rooted in Black culture. Obama moves to his second telling comment: "I do apologize. I know I was a little late tonight. I was running on CPT, which stands for jokes that White people should not make." As the crowd erupts, he and Wilmore, again, connect eyes. In skewering Bill de Blasio and Hillary Clinton for making a joke about Black culture that wasn't theirs to make, Obama is also simultaneously giving his blessings to Wilmore to do exactly that. Within his first minute, Obama seems to be saying, as he so often does, "Let me be clear": Get ready, because we are about to hear about race, and from someone who has the right to do so.

And when Wilmore (2016a) takes the mic, he boldly follows suit. Typically, anything related to media and politics is fair game at WHCDs; however, Wilmore, unlike previous comedians, intertwines artistic and social choices that are pointedly about matters of race and Black culture. He opens with "Welcome to 'Negro Night' here at the Washington Hilton, or as Fox News will report, 'Two thugs disrupt elegant dinner in D.C.' That's how they do us, right?" and he and Obama share yet another knowing smirk. And he just rolls from there: Wilmore gives voice to cocoa butter, Black Jesus, *Sanford and Son*; he mentions Black Lives Matters four times, refers to Becky with the good hair, jigaboos, and Black Panthers. The audience, mostly White, mostly squirms in spite of their own laughter.

After 20 minutes, Wilmore concludes with one last joke about voting for Obama solely because he is Black, and remaining his supporter, regardless of his policies, so long as he is still Black. Wilmore then drops his comedic posturing and quite tenderly expresses, speaking directly to Obama, the historical implication that his presidency means to him as a Black man. Wilmore concludes his heartfelt message with "Words alone do me no justice. So, Mr. President, if I'm going to keep it 100: Yo, Barry, you did it, my n–ga. You did it."

Wilmore's use of the n-word instantly fills the room with uncertainty and also immediately goes viral on social media, with everyone expressing their opinion on its propriety. But in that public moment that is extremely intimate, when Wilmore fist-pumps his chest, and Obama does likewise as he stands to hug Wilmore, we witness not only a comedian and a president embracing but also two Black men—Larry and Barry—rooted in affection, rooted in a lineage that is transforming in this very performative moment. Indeed, the n-word is a volatile word, loaded with historical implications and frequently used to take away or disparage the identity of Blacks, but Wilmore's "artistic choice" is to intentionally expose the truthful beauty that lies under the layers of hatred that Whites have created for the Black race with this word and to provide a "show of affection that only we can understand" (Wilmore, 2016b). And I contend that Wilmore was inspired to be authentic, to keep it 100, from witnessing the sustained racio-rhetoric of his president. Their warm embrace was a communication not only with each other but with other Black men as well. For many Blacks, particularly Black men, this exchange is a moment of enormous pride. Capturing this sentiment, blogger and TV producer Williams (2016) wrote, "what we witnessed Saturday night were two Black men who did not care that white people were present," calling it "a fiercely political moment."

Obama's legacy: Keeping it 100

As Obama ends his two-term presidency, we can itemize his considerable influence in multiple directions: our economy; our environment; health care; civil rights for the lesbian, gay, bisexual, and transgender, and women communities; foreign policy; homeland security; along with endless attempts to reduce gun violence and fulfill the ninth seat of the Supreme Court. His accomplishments are indeed impressive.

But beyond this political legacy, Obama also contributes to our country's historical tradition of thinking about the materiality of Black men and Black men's lives, a centuries-old tradition. Franklin (1994), a pioneer in men's studies, eloquently reminds us that "Black masculinities in the United States began their development as 'the boat' inched closer to Jamestown" (p. 4). Masculinity and masculine identities, however, are constantly shifting and reconstructing, and Obama—through his performances of masculinity and his intentional use of humor—has provided a healthy, fresh addition to our historical store of knowledge.

Over the last 8+ years, Obama has demonstrated a consistently tangible and emancipatory means for Black men to communicate with both authenticity and agency by using rhetorical comedy that simultaneously disrupts troublesome constructions and representations while rearticulating a masculinity that is truthful and effective. And like every brilliant rhetorician, Obama knows his audience and how best to reach them. One of Obama's understated tools of comedy, and we've certainly seen it at the WHCDs, is his use of asides; while the live audience, who is predominantly White, is rapt with laughter, he utters, almost imperceptibly, little follow-up comments—"somebody's gotta do it," "that's right," "mm-mm-mm," "settle down"—as if he were doing call-and-response to his own comedy, as if replacing the feedback were he in front of a Black audience. Although these asides may barely register with his live audience, his fellow Blacks—who are digitally watching him later—are rhetorically and culturally locked in. When Obama is performing both comedy and masculinity, he is intentionally keeping it 100, always, and he is fully aware that not just Key and Peele, not just Larry Wilmore, not just professional comedians, but a nation of Black men are watching him, and more so, they are identifying with him, learning from him, and modeling after him.

References

CNN. (2015). *CNN/ORC international poll*. Retrieved from http://i2.cdn.turner.com/cnn/2015/images/09/12/iranpoll.pdf

Connell, R. W. (1995). *Masculinities*. Oakland, CA: University of California Press.

Cooper, F. R. (2003). Cultural context matters: Terry's "seesaw effect." *Oklahoma Law Review, 56*, 833–878.

Ehlers, N. (2012). *Racial imperatives: Discipline, performativity, and struggles against subjection*. Bloomington, IN: Indiana University Press.

Franklin, C. W. (1994). Men's studies, the men's movement, and the study of Black masculinities: Further demystification of masculinities in America. In R.G. Majors & J. U. Gordon (Eds.), *The American Black male: His present status and his future* (pp. 3–19). Chicago, IL: Nelson-Hall.

Galifianakis, Z. (2014, March 11). *Between two ferns with Zach Galifianakis: President Barack Obama* (Episode 18) [Web series]. Retrieved from http://www.funnyordie.com/between_two_ferns

Jackson, R. L. (2006). *Scripting the Black masculine body: Identity, discourse, and racial politics in popular media*. Albany, NY: State University of New York Press.

Johnson, A. J. (1997). *The gender knot: Unraveling our patriarchal legacy*. Philadelphia: Temple University Press.

Lichter, S. R., Baumgartner, J. C., & Morris, J. C. (2015). *Politics is a joke! How TV comedians are remaking political life*. Boulder, CO: Westview Press.

Key, K.-M. (2012, February 8). Interview by C. O'Brien. *Conan* [Television broadcast]. New York, NY: TBS.

Key, K.-M. (2015, August 15). Interview by J. Fallon. *The Tonight Show with Jimmy Fallon* [Television broadcast]. New York, NY: NBC.

Kimmell, M. (2011). *Manhood in America: A cultural history*. (3rd ed.). Oxford, England: Oxford University Press.

Majors, R., & Billson, J. M. (1992). *Cool pose: The dilemmas of Black manhood in America*. New York, NY: Lexington Books.

McGhee, P. E. (1979). *Humor: Its origins and development*. San Francisco, CA: W. H. Freeman.

Meyer, J. C. (2000). Humor as a double-edged sword: Four functions of humor in communication. *Communication Theory, 10*, 310–331.

Meyer, J. C. (2015). *Understanding humor through communication: Why be funny, anyway?* Lanham, MD: Lexington Books.

Meyers, S. (2011, April 14). Interview by D. Letterman. *Late Show with David Letterman* [Television broadcast]. New York, NY: CBS.

Morreall, J. (1983). *Taking laughter seriously*. Albany, NY: State University of New York Press.

Obama, B. (1995). *Dreams from my father: A story of race and inheritance*. New York, NY: Times Books.

Obama, B. (2006). *The audacity of hope: Thoughts on reclaiming the American dream*. New York, NY: Random House.

Obama, B. (2011, April). Remarks presented at 2011 White House Correspondents Dinner, Washington, DC.

Obama, B. (2012, April 25). Interview by J. Fallon. *The Tonight Show with Jimmy Fallon* [Television broadcast]. New York, NY: NBC.

Obama, B. (2015a, April). Remarks presented at 2015 White House Correspondents Dinner, Washington, DC.

Obama, B. (2015b, June 22). *WTF with Marc Maron*. (No. 613) [Audio podcast]. Retrieved from http://www.wtfpod.com/podcast/episodes/episode_613_-_president_barack_obama

Obama, B. (2016, April). Remarks presented at 2016 White House Correspondents Dinner, Washington, DC. Retrieved from https://www.c-span.org/2016-White-House-Correspondents-Association-Dinner/

Obeidallah, D. (2016, April 30). Barack Obama, comedian in chief. *The Atlantic*. Retrieved from http://www.theatlantic.com/politics/archive/2016/04/barack-obama-killer-comedian-in-chief/480441/

Rossing, J. P. (2011). Comic provocations in racial culture: Barack Obama and the "Politics of Fear." *Communication Studies, 62*, 422–438.

Seinfeld, J. (2015, December 30). "Just tell him you're the president" (S7 E1). *Comedians in Cars Getting Coffee* [Web series]. Retrieved from http://comediansincarsgettingcoffee.com/president-barack-obama-just-tell-him-you-re-the-president

Shaw, M. E., & Watson, E. (2011). Obama's masculinities: A landscape of essential contradictions. In E. Watson & M.E. Shaw (Eds.), *Performing American masculinities: The 21st-century man in popular culture* (pp. 134–152). Bloomington, IN: Indiana University Press.

Waisanen, D. (2015). Comedian-in-chief: Presidential jokes as enthymematic crisis rhetoric. *Presidential Studies Quarterly, 45*, 335–360.

Williams, E. W. (2016, May 2). What it means when Larry Wilmore calls President Obama "my nigga." *Vice*. Retrieved from http://www.vice.com/en_ca/read/what-it-means-when-larry-wilmore-calls-president-obama-my-nigga

Wilmore, L. (host). (2015). *The Nightly Show with Larry Wilmore* [Television series]. Retrieved from http://www.cc.com/video-clips/9x15nr/the-nightly-show-with-larry-wilmore-obama-don-t-care—the-first-lady-is-rapping

Wilmore, L. (2016a, April). Remarks presented at 2016 White House Correspondents Dinner, Washington, DC. Retrieved from https://www.c-span.org/video/?c4589542/larry-wilmore-complete-remarks-2016-whca-dinner

Wilmore, L. (2016b, May 3). Interview by T. Gross. *Fresh air* [Radio broadcast]. Philadelphia, PA: NPR.

Image Control: The Visual Rhetoric of President Obama

Timothy R. Gleason and Sara S. Hansen

> **ABSTRACT**
> President Barack Obama was elected upon a wave of change he described as "hope." On the front of image control, the Obama administration has offered little hope in providing greater access to information compared to previous administrations, exemplified by the exclusion of photojournalists from a number of events. Using Althusser's Ideological State Apparatus and visual rhetoric, this analysis examines the process of image control and interprets official photographs from these events to argue against such practices. Findings suggest that photographer exclusion altered media rituals, allowed through White House power to change its relationship with the press and communicate directly with the public through new media channels. Image control seen in analyzed photographs produced mundane perspectives and presidential legitimacy conveyed in symbols and meanings that reinforce norms, and potentially lessen impact of race. Implications for Obama's legacy and future White House practices are discussed.

President Barack Obama upset photojournalists in 2013 by not permitting them to photograph events that have traditionally been photographed. Instead of allowing coverage, the White House released photographs made by Obama's own chief photographer, Pete Souza, and deputy photographer, Chuck Kennedy. Obama's spokesman, Jay Carney, was challenged by reporters regarding this practice, and some members of the press refused to use Souza's photographs until photojournalists were given the same access they had previously experienced. Carney had countered that the Internet and social media channels enabled the White House to share images directly with the public, and the press responded that the public is given only one perspective in this communication flow. To address this attempted image control, this study looks at the system of image control, the visual rhetoric of the images, and potential motivations for this control surrounding modern political image management.

Importantly, Obama represents the celebrity human brand that generates authenticity with voters and funding from endorsers (Thomson, 2006). This authenticity is contrasted with strategic use of image control, such as visually aligning with the

John F. Kennedy ideal to build upon public discourses (Frame, 2012). The system of image control is analyzed partly through Louis Althusser's (2014) concept of the ideological state apparatus (ISA). The ISA is the means by which the controlling power tries to project its ideas onto the public. The press can be a significant player in the ISA, either as a participant or a challenger. The existence of the Obama-as-celebrity phenomenon also functions within the perspective of the ISA framework. Photographs are used to communicate ideas, so it is not surprising that the elites attempt to maintain control over representations of those in power (Boorstin, 1962; Gleason, 2005). Such images may help or hurt a cultivated political celebrity persona. Obama's celebrity status has drawn critique from opponents in both of his presidential runs (Steinhauser, 2012). However, the president's strong media visibility with this celebrity has enabled him to promote his agenda in the United States (Kellner, 2009). As his term effectively ends in 2016, Obama's impression management aims to positively support his legacy. Post-Obama, this management strategically supports advancement of the Democratic Party from its most visible leader and first president to successfully leverage "social brand building" to win the White House (Mac, 2012).

A visual rhetoric analysis of images distributed by the White House when the visual press was not present can explain symbolic representations the administration wanted to communicate to the public, necessitated through altered practices of activity and interaction with the media as seen in Anthony Giddens' Structuration Theory (Giddens, 1993; den Hond, Boersma, Heres, Kroes, & van Oirschot, 2012). Potentially, this analysis aligns with presidential and political-party impression management. The data analyzed is a set of photos made by White House photographers and posted on the White House Flickr account at http://www.flickr.com/photos/whitehouse.

Literature review

The context of photojournalism routine

"Presidents stage photo-opportunities to influence, manipulate, entreat, entice, amaze, or otherwise assume power over witnesses" (Erickson, 2000, p. 139), but times change with technological innovation and social conditions. For photojournalists on the White House beat, the move to exclude them is a disruption to their routine. Broadly, these routines are part of journalism operations. Scholars have offered different ways of considering how journalism works to present news, such as gatekeeping (e.g., Stempel, 1985; Shoemaker, 1991), and news production from a "complex organization" (Tuchman, 1978). A photojournalist may ask, If I have covered certain types of events before in my job, why not now?

The White House is, in effect, saying photojournalists are not needed in particular scenarios because the news sharing routine can be circumvented with online galleries and Flickr. Arguably, public expectations of photo content and quality are shifting with the growing presence of amateur photography and citizen journalism capturing photographic or newsworthy moments. Users may immediately share photos with ease on social network sites such as Facebook, Twitter, Instagram, and others, especially as photography becomes "ubiquitous" (Hand, 2012). Yet, citizen journalism is not the same as professional photojournalism, particularly in terms of quality, integrity, breadth, storytelling, and reliability (Garcia, 2012).

Further, the repeated disruption to practices, routines, and rituals may signal a shift in the Obama administration's management of its images, presidential branding, and storytelling that connects image projections to performance or reputation. Brand management may minimize inconsistencies between a projected brand identity and an externally validated brand reputation (De Chernatony, 1999). By partially changing procedures for some events, the administration gains control of image projections to help tell its own story to the American and global public.

Nick Couldry (2003) defined *media rituals* as "formalised actions organised around key media-related categories and boundaries, whose performance frames, or suggests a connection with, wider media-related values" (p. 29). Americans value freedom and access to information, but most people are not aware that White House access is a media ritual. Obama's "symbolic power" lies in his ability to maintain this media ritual—controlled access to photograph certain events—and let the media convey the representation crafted in the White House. His symbolic power also enables him to prohibit access to White House events (Couldry, 2003, p. 39). den Hond et al. (2012) noted how structuration relies on reproduction or repetitive practices in these systems that demonstrate power, which suggests a relationship between ritual and maintenance of the structure.

Althusser's ISA

The notion that governments actively attempt to orient populations around ruling ideas is widely accepted. In an interview, Noam Chomsky (Peck, 1987) called such efforts the "engineering of consent" and "thought control" (p. 49). Herbert I. Schiller (1989) wrote, "The informational question, in all its dimensions—practical and theoretical—is an urgent political issue in America. ... what is seen, heard, and read—is worsening steadily" (p. 164). Daniel J. Boorstin (1962) wrote on "pseudo-events" as the use of persuasive images in politics, and the emerging celebrity culture. Countless others have speculated on the relationships between politics, ideology, press, and images. The challenge in outlining these relationships stems from the constantly shifting sands of these parts, but there is little argument that political authorities have a vested interest in creating messages that support the maintenance of their power, as well as its increase.

In discussing theorists who do not recognize the degree of agency "subordinate classes" have at their disposal, Giddens identified Althusser (Giddens, 1993, pp. 124–125). Althusser's ISA offers benefits to the analysis of government and the press. It explains different forms of coercion the government has at its disposal, including the repressive state apparatus (RSA). The value of considering Althusser's work is the recognition that ideology serves to reinforce the ideas of the powerful, but behind the ideology is a specter of violence. Images of a president can be read as the leader of the country taking charge for our benefit, in addition to the holder of mechanisms of state-sanctioned repression. For Althusser (2014),

> An ideological state apparatus is a system of defined institutions, organizations, and the corresponding practices. Realized in the institutions, organizations, and practices of this system is all or part (generally speaking, a typical combination of certain elements) of the State Ideology. The ideology realized in an ISA ensures its systemic unity on the basis of an 'anchoring' in material functions specific to each ISA: these functions are not reducible to that ideology, but serve it as a "support." (p. 77)

Althusser (2014) composed a "provisional list" of apparatuses that fall under the umbrella of the ISA, and this list includes "Scholastic," "Familial," and "Information and News Apparatus" (p. 75). These are not repressive because they do not function on the basis of violence, or the potential of it. Instead, they are apparatuses that people often actively participate in, such as going to classes, reading news, attending church, and watching movies (Althusser, 2014). Althusser argued against the significant differentiation between concepts of the public and private because they can both serve the state (i.e., doing the work of those in control to spread its ruling ideology).

The broad notion of celebrity in American culture—film, music, politics, reality television—also may be listed as an apparatus. Just as citizen journalism has welcomed the average person to a public stage, a celebrity culture now welcomes the idea that anyone can be famous through a reality television show or viral video. The prevalence and fascination of celebrity on large and small screens in U.S. culture broadly supports an "expectation" of celebrity in political image too. For example, modern politicians take the stage on late-night and comedy television, including *The Daily Show* and *Saturday Night Live*. By Althusser's framework, citizens' pre-set expectation for celebrity supports this presence in public, always-on sources of traditional and new media. These ideologically state-set ideals or expectations citizens embrace as their own, making celebrity status appealing for presidents and other politicians.

Citizens often play their assigned roles in a capitalist state by, as President George W. Bush famously suggested, consuming goods. In a critical-cultural analysis, Katherine Bell (2011) evaluated the use of celebrity in the Product RED cause-marketing campaign to fight AIDS in Africa. This work evaluated race, celebrity, and consumerism encouraged by major celebrities and brands that generated consumer purchases with proceeds to support a cause. Bell draws upon Bourdieu's (1991) hierarchical representation of celebrity as symbolic, economic, and cultural capital that allows individuals to distinguish others in different social fields. The campaign used celebrity to connect consumers with desired identity imposed by power holders. With Althusser's interpellation, Bell describes Product RED with opposing forces of poverty (in Africa imagery) and consumption (an American solution to raise funds) that invite and hail citizens as "it summons the consumer subject to use his/her buying power for social good … We are 'always already' subjects in capitalism, habituated by the social and state apparatuses that allow for consumption to be taken up with seemingly contradictory discourses" (p. 170).

The "always already" citizen welcomes the celebrity president. However, the image of celebrity is crafted from the bureaucratic field where symbolic capital works only with those who can perceive, via shared culture understanding, what the symbols mean (Bourdieu, Wacquant, & Farage, 1994). Matthew Thomson (2006) found human brands succeed when reinforcing consumers' feelings of autonomy and relatedness without threatening feelings of competency. Arguably, symbols understood broadly by society help human brands reinforce these ideas.

The use of popular culture and social media adds to political symbolic communication. Co-creation between celebrities and consumers' identities (Banister & Cocker, 2014) happens within a participatory culture (Jenkins, 2006) that increasingly offers consumer experiences via direct and interactive communication in fan-based and social media. Obama, successfully harnessing these new channels, opened such symbolic dialogue and image-making that engaged Americans in their terms with two-way media. He is the first U.S. president who does not need to rely solely on traditional media, press coverage, and photojournalism to reinforce, aligned with Thomson (2006), citizens' perceived ideals:

> Obama articulated an image of himself as an inspiring political authority who does not expect a 'blind' or rationally motivated form of obedience. He spoke about authority as a reciprocal and communicative, two-way, power relationship that combines goals, tactics, and ethos in order to get people with different, and sometimes even incompatible, identities and projects freely to accept that cooperation across all conventional boundaries may be the only way to resolve the common challenges and problems of the United States and the world in general. (Bang, 2009, p. 133)

Exploratory research questions

The Obama administration changed press access in limited situations that disrupted news-gathering routines and allowed for some control over the production of messages. These actions depart from long-standing traditions of the White House and democratic practice. Practices and routines between institutions and the media are influenced through powerful institutions that exert ideologies in societal apparatuses, such as news and political systems, celebrity, and consumerism. Symbolic communication that engages citizens toward desired institutional goals may maintain power relationships. This is important because the symbols and meanings are used by those in power to maintain power, largely by communicating authority to exert power, by representing power-holders as having an inherent right to power, and by contrasting the righteousness of those in power to others who are represented as being well served by the political structure. Considering the potential goals of the White House in changing access for photojournalism practices that excludes the media, two research questions are posed.

> RQ1: What is the nature of the press-excluded events conveyed in White House photos?
> RQ2: What are the symbols and meanings conveyed in White House photos from press-excluded events?

Table 1. Image descriptions with White House Flickr URLs.

Description	URL
Image 1: July 10, 2013, Obama meets with members of Congressional Hispanic Caucus	http://www.flickr.com/photos/whitehouse/9255382759/
Image 2: July 11, 2013, Obama meets with Chinese representatives	https://www.flickr.com/photos/whitehouse/9263319497/
Image 3: July 11, 2013, after the meeting with Chinese representatives	https://www.flickr.com/photos/whitehouse/9526191484/
Image 4: July 11, 2013, after the meeting with Chinese representative	http://www.flickr.com/photos/whitehouse/9523407969/
Image 5: July 29, 2013, Obama meets with former Secretary of State Hillary Clinton	https://www.flickr.com/photos/whitehouse/9523406827/
Image 6: July 29, 2013, Obama meets with former Secretary of State Hillary Clinton	https://www.flickr.com/photos/whitehouse/9392996813/
Image 7: July 30, 2013, Obama and Biden meet with Israeli and Palestinian negotiators	https://www.flickr.com/photos/whitehouse/9403801570/
Image 8: August 26, 2013, Obama meets with African-American faith leaders	https://www.flickr.com/photos/whitehouse/9602894286/ https://www.flickr.com/photos/whitehouse/9658815276/
Image 9: September 2, 2013, Obama meets with Senators McCain and Graham.	http://worldnews.nbcnews.com/_news/2013/10/11/20926391-pakistani-girl-malala-yousafzai-meets-obamas-at-white-house
Image 10: October 11, 2013, Obama and his family meet with Malala Yousafzai.	This photo is now only found on news sites

Method

Images posted online from the White House depicting events without photojournalists, which were outlined in a letter of protest to Jay Carney,[1] were evaluated. Ten images (see Table 1) were analyzed using the ISA framework and visual rhetoric toward projecting ideas of the state to the public with symbolic meanings. Using purposive sampling, images were selected to represent different subjects in the news (e.g., African-American leaders, officials from Israel and Palestine, and Hillary Clinton), in a handful of different locations in and outside the White House and representing different races and genders. Most significantly, these were situations when photojournalists were excluded from events, and the only visual representations available to the public were those provided by the White House. The study's themes emerge from this analysis.

Visual rhetoric

Visual rhetoric is an analytical tool for interpreting a variety of forms of material culture, especially photographs, for the symbolic representations that promote and challenge existing structures. It has become somewhat of a blanket term in communication studies because scholars apply their own interpretive framework to photographs, so two scholars may produce two readings of the same images. Images contain messages to be interpreted through the organization of visual elements. Meanings are made through exploration of the image in social, cultural, political, and economic contexts, as well as knowledge of how the image was made. It is the obligation of scholars to defend their arguments because the methodology is scholar-centric. Visual rhetoric has been influenced by art criticism that is underpinned by knowledge of image production and rhetorical analysis that approaches a visual text the same as the written text. The visual rhetoric of media images has been explored, most notably, by Robert Hariman and John Louis Lucaites (2007), Diane Hope (2006), and Lester C. Olson (2008).

A visual rhetoric's qualitative methodology has inherent strengths and weaknesses. Visual rhetoric allows for interpretation that may differ among researchers. The researcher determines the sampling based on the subject matter, rather than a one-size-fits-all system. Purposive sampling is used to look at particular images, subjects, or some specific category. "When your research purpose requires that particular messages or behaviors or people be studied, you are not interested in generalizing your findings to an entire population of messages, behaviors, or people" (Merrigan & Huston, 2004, p. 43). The nature of a purposive sampling is that the communicative product or text has qualities of interest, such as embodying a trend or a break from past practices. Terry Barrett (2012) has discussed how critics have selected images for interpretation with the assumption an image needs interpretation, "Another way of understanding interpretation is to think of all photographs as metaphors in need of being deciphered" (p. 49).

Analysis of press-excluded photos

As evident in the case of the White House exclusions, the State does not license the press to operate; but it de facto licenses it by choosing who can cover what in the White House. To borrow from the language of Stuart Hall (1980), the administration can reduce the number of possible encoded meanings—although not the decoded meanings—by excluding photojournalists. The images provided by the White House have meanings encoded in them, and these need to be interpreted within the context of their construction—that is, the images were the products of an active agent (White House photographer Souza) working not just as part of the ISA, but working for those who try to maintain control of the ISA.

A visual rhetoric analysis of images explains the meaning of the images as communicative devices. The White House's photographs are visual artifacts meant for viewer consumption. According to Hope (2006), "Visual artifacts provoke intended and unintended meanings for individual and collective identity, and they begin with processes of perception" (p. 5).

This analysis was conducted with the assumption that White House images from press-excluded events were chosen because of specific visual elements that communicate preferred meanings. By looking at the individual images and then looking at them as a set, themes emerge that create a visual rhetoric. Considering the press was excluded, it is likely the White House had common concerns about having the visual press attend, excluded them for those reasons, and provided images that reflected a promoted visual rhetoric. The short time people spend viewing images would prohibit the subtle inclusion of visual elements that did not already have meaning. This is not to suggest that people are simple or unable to come to their own conclusions. Instead, people are in a hurry and do not intentionally read for encoded meanings, so the White House image-makers present scenes that are oriented toward a particular reading. This is what Hall (1980) called the "hegemonic" position.

Timothy R. Gleason (2005) argued visual rhetoric analysis should accept the premise that people who engage with images will not interpret them in the same way, especially as intended. Using Hall's reception analysis, Gleason (2005) agreed people may accept, negotiate, or oppose messages' "encoded" meanings. Hariman and Lucaites (2007) phrased it as, "Because the 'same' image can already contain within it both dominant and resistant responses to social authority, there need not be just one effect" (p. 10). Messages are "decoded" by people with their pre-existing beliefs and values, which impact the reading of images. Gleason (2005) suggested photojournalists produce an alternative visual rhetoric that does not place authority in the hands of politicians in an effort to seek a best-possible truth—a fair representation of people, space, and context—within the confines created by image-handlers.

Results

The nature of press-excluded events

In terms of RQ1, White House portrayals in the press-excluded events appeared to show business as usual in mundane and non-standout ways. Depictions of these events in the analyzed photos exhibited little creative treatment. Images often showed subjects within a larger view of rooms and people cast from a similar distance. They did not show close-up images, unique elements of focus or other creative treatments that could be at the discretion of photojournalists.

The White House photos are mostly interior images—both literally and figuratively. Most of them were taken inside the White House, but they also represent the effort to protect Obama's image. In a number of these images, the rooms contain visual representations of past American political and social leaders that serve to encourage the viewer to connect Obama with the individuals. Photo properties convey leadership and power displays that vary in scenes of the Oval Office, White House meeting rooms, and neutral backdrops like nondescript rooms or gardens. The proprietary photographing shows a low-risk, mundane effort to craft an image of Obama in people's minds. Lastly, Obama shines in some carefree moments when he can be less formal (see Table 1, Image 4) and with children, as seen in other official White House Flickr images. Ironically, the White House press office seemingly pushed the cardboard caricature of Obama that has hurt his likeability, and at a time of worsening poll results (Sullivan, 2013).

Overall, the photos align with the following statement. "President Barack Obama was frequently portrayed as a thoughtful leader who generally maintained a professional distance from those he interacted with at the White House during meetings, but this representation is occasionally offset by images of him at ease." Findings in terms of RQ2 are presented within three themes that show distinct image location as backdrop combined with meanings of artifacts.

Symbols and meanings in White House photos

Hospitality in the Oval Office: Freedom fighting on stage with American symbolism

Obama was frequently photographed inside the White House where he met with various people. A common location was the Oval Office, where Obama would sit in the same leather chair. When Vice President Joe Biden is in the picture, Biden sits at Obama's right. When Biden is absent, the important guest sits in Biden's chair (see Table 1, Images 2, 7, 9, and 10). Two sofas face each other and are positioned seemingly perpendicular to the plane running across the Obama and Biden chairs. Guests on the sofas have to turn to their right or left, depending on the sofa, to see the president. Behind and above Obama is a portrait of President George Washington situated above a fireplace, and visible on the left side of the frame is a portrait of President Abraham Lincoln. Between them is a bust of Martin Luther King, Jr., resting on a table, and above the bust is a copy of the Emancipation Proclamation.

The direction taken by White House photographers is one likely to be taken by many photojournalists, although photojournalists may also try to create more unexpected images. The more generic images are frequently treated as safe shots by photojournalists because they know they have a usable photograph from that perspective, but a perspective that is not unique or radical. The safe shot provides a historical narrative. The presence of Washington is fundamental in establishing the location of Obama's whereabouts, the city was named after him, and Washington figures prominently in the idea of the presidency. The relationship between President Obama and President Washington is not one of parity. Washington watches over Obama, exemplified by the high position of his portrait above the fireplace. Washington serves as a reminder that Obama is president, but it also communicates the idea that Obama is following in the footsteps of the first president. The challenge for Obama is overcoming that difference between the legendary Washington and the struggling Obama.

The portrait of Lincoln is positioned lower than the one of Washington. The top of the Lincoln picture frame is at about the same height as the middle of the Washington picture frame. The lower position can be seen as an act of deference to Washington, who was more of a hero throughout the north and south than Lincoln was during each man's time. Although Obama may sit in front of Washington, he frequently has to look in Lincoln's direction. In the White House's photos Obama tends to look to his right and would be aware of the Lincoln portrait. Obama would be aware of the presence of Lincoln more than Washington during the events from which the photographs emerged. Between Lincoln and Obama are the King bust and Emancipation Proclamation copy. The construct of the Oval Office photographs tends to reinforce freedom in obvious ways, although it is difficult to tell that the document on the wall is the Emancipation Proclamation copy. Nevertheless, the representations of men all pour into a basin of freedom.

Thus, Obama is portrayed as the next generation to fight for freedom, and he is also suggested to be the product of the fight for freedom. His presidency would not have been possible without the leadership of these three men. In a way, he is a transcendent figure who has been led and now leads. This idea is stronger when a viewer associates Obama with the three wise men, but accordingly weaker when a viewer sees a difference between Obama and the men. Perception, as we know, is in the value-system of the beholder.

In most of the Oval Office photos taken during different seasons there is a bowl of apples on a table between the two sofas and not far from Obama. The apples can symbolize different things to different people, as the nature of symbols is that their meanings or associations can vary based on a person's own values and experiences (Barthes, 1973; Hall, 1980). Of the fruits, the apple family is seemingly one of the most American kinds (e.g., "As American as apple pie"). The apple also represents good health (e.g., "An apple a day keeps the doctor away"), as well as kindness (e.g., giving an apple to a teacher). More controversially is its association with good and evil. An apple tree is in the Garden of Eden but the apples are not to be eaten. The presence of the apples is more open to interpretation than may be first thought. Optimistic viewers may see the apples in a positive light because they input their own positive associations with this visual relationship. The apples are provided as gifts to his guests because they offer health and knowledge. Conversely, those already positioned to oppose Obama may see the apples as the temptation associated with sin. For those who see Obama as an un-American Muslim, they may see the symbolic value of apples as the taste of eternal sin. Objects may contain the essence of ambiguity more than others, and apples are a subtle pushing point to either side.

In these photos the president is frequently appearing distant or impersonal, as if the intended representation is to reinforce a more classic view of masculine leadership. However, the meaning is impacted by the political context of Obama being criticized as too stoic and unemotional. By using a traditional form of distance-as-masculinity, the images only reinforce the emergent stereotype of the president as too analytical or robotic.

Leadership in large meeting rooms: Contrasts of the affable and unemotional

In office and meeting room settings the president is frequently represented as in charge and easily visible. Sometimes other people are cropped out, their faces are not as visible or their presence is nearly overtaken by the presence of the table with apples. In these images, the president is the subject, even when the guests are notable, such as Senator John McCain and Pakistani child and author Malala Yousafzai (see Table 1, Images 9 and 10). Interestingly, Obama is treated less as a subject in the images with faith leaders from August 26, 2013 (see Table 1, Image 8). It is somewhat difficult to find Obama in a room with 19 visible individuals, although his profile is his homing beacon. Obama is so pushed to the far right of the frame—apparently to show more people present—he becomes tucked away in the crowd. He gestures as he speaks—again controlling the room—but he becomes one person among many in the Roosevelt Room. The attendees are listening intently with name cards situated before them and not one person appears to have chosen to keep a glass of water nearby, although a pitcher of water is visible in the left edge of the frame. What appear to be the two youngest members of the group sit on a sofa near the table where most attendees are sitting. They are apart not just by location but also by age. The Roosevelt Room is interesting because, at least in this image, it has a portrait of Franklin D. Roosevelt sitting and one of Rough Rider Teddy Roosevelt on his galloping horse. It is a contrast of two men. Teddy's activity reminds us of FDR's health problems. This contrast increases the apparent differences between the people at the table—mainly older men—and the younger man and woman on the sofa. The latter's presence make the older men appear even more aged. The increasingly grayer Obama begins to look more like the elders at the table than the seemingly young man who first ran for president. The men who enter the White House as president always appear to age disproportionately at their exit.

In one way it is an odd photograph. This is an exceptional moment in history with a mixed-race president entertaining faith leaders who are predominately African American, yet the image is somber. It suggests serious discussion, but the moment offers so much hope for the future. The caption explains the group met to talk about education, health care, and jobs. It is a reminder that the problems of the past still exist, so it appears no joy can be taken in the moment.

In contrast, Obama appears as the most important man in the room with the Chinese delegation in a July 11, 2013 photo (see Table 1, Image 2). Obama gestures as he looks to his right and speaks with a representative, who has his fingers interlocked and his legs bent straight down. Obama looks at ease and in command as others watch him or take notes. The Chinese illustrate uniformity and redundancy when looking at the minor subjects. The three men on the left are all positioned nearly identically, which reinforces the historic criticism of the lack of individuality in China. Each man sits like the man neighboring Obama, but they each lean forward as if each was being captured by his words.

The meeting photo is strikingly different than an image of Obama shaking hands with Chinese Vice Premier Wang Yang while a woman gazes at Obama (see Table 1, Image 3). Although taken slightly from behind the profile, it is obvious Obama offers a big smile as others in the room laugh. This is an engaging photo and the kind photojournalists would likely aim for because it is a distinctive moment in time that departs from the mundane. The actors are humanized by their display of personality that gives hope to the possibility of a better relationship between the two countries. The caption states it follows the meeting to suggest the participants were happy the meeting was over and/or pleased with its results.

Viewed together, the pairing shows a more well-rounded representation of the meeting. Viewing one image without the other simplifies the visual message of Obama as the leader but a distant leader, or Obama as the affable host who puts his guests at ease. The more Obama is represented in formal interaction, the less comfortable he appears. This may seem logical (How many of us feel uncomfortable in these situations?), but these are the selections made by the White House communications office that further reinforces the memory image of Obama as the unemotional president. The White House can define the president's signification in these images, yet the images frequently reinforce the cold Obama over the warm, interactive Obama.

Neutral spaces to share power: "Old friends" symbolically meet in the middle
The friendly Obama is visible in the July 29, 2013 lunch photo with Hillary Clinton, where they sit outdoors eating salads. Clinton and Obama are both laughing with Clinton looking at Obama, while Obama looks down at his silverware (see Table 1, Image 6). An empty chair between them is set back into the shadows produced by trees. In the background is bright light that pulls attention away from the subject, at times. It is an image that surprises when considering they competed for the 2008 Democratic nomination. This suggests that their time working together—Clinton as Obama's secretary of state—patched the cuts and healed the bruises from campaigning against each other. Viewers are reminded of her supporting role in his return to the White House (see Table 1, Image 5). It can also be read as a sign of support as rumors persist at the time that Clinton will attempt a second presidential run. Aesthetically, the image has its problems because of the trees and light in the background. The image shows a lightness missing in the meeting shots, further suggesting the weight of the presidency on Obama. Again, he appears as two men—sometimes warm and energetic, and other times worn by his leadership.

Image controls and conflicts

Viewing all of the photos in this selection, a broader control of image may be seen in how Obama is positioned related to other people to convey dominant or equalized power. Obama is cast as the prominent figure in all of the photos except for the two pictures with Clinton, and the respective photos with African American leaders and Israeli-Palestinian negotiators. Does this equalization mean to extend brand identity of the president toward performance or reputation? Equalization with Clinton may signal a shared power, perhaps to transfer presidential status or deference for party leadership as the former First Lady considers a 2016 presidential run (see Table 1, Image 5). Being a part of the crowd—sharing space with other groups—may symbolize a shared responsibility to support and help pose solutions related to African American domestic issues, or Middle-Eastern peace. Obama's performance as a leader of shared responsibility potentially alters expectations of how the Obama brand is faring in terms of public opinion. Indeed, Obama directed Secretary of State John Kerry to push negotiations forward with the Palestinians and Israelis, which started the day the photograph was taken. As well, the meeting of African American leaders was on the anniversary of the march on Washington, and the people attending and the topics according to the caption represented the past and the future. In both cases, the symbolic meetings appear to support Obama's priorities.

This selection of images shows the conflict of Obama projected depictions. The contrast becomes even greater when reviewing the White House's Flickr photostream, which shows many spontaneous moments the president had with his guests, especially children. He appears unencumbered by the weight of the presidency when he is with children. Being president is a serious job and meetings with politicians and other public figures are not to be taken lightly, but Obama never appears at ease during these times. He becomes himself when the political situations evaporate. He plays chase with a little girl around his desk on April 12, 2013; he helps a boy with a tie and jacket before a departure photo on May 10, 2013; and he adjusts a picture frame in the Lower Press Office while a press assistant appears to laugh.[2]

It is unfair to expect Obama to be light when the moments are not, but the White House chooses to release these photographs to the public without the participation of independent photojournalists. The White House attempts to define the parameters of the discourse when it really cannot achieve this aim, because individuals impute their own views into interpretation of the images. The exclusion of the photojournalists from some quite mundane events may do little to change the historical record of these events, but it does do significantly more in crafting the perception of the White House as almost paranoid in its image management. When politicians work in the darkness, the public imagines what they are not seeing.

Discussion

This analysis of the White House's attempts to limit representations of the president uses Althusser's (2014) ISA as a framework to interpret the visual rhetoric constructed by the Obama presidency, regarded as an activity of structuration. As each aspect has been considered rather independently, it is beneficial to step back and look at how they work together. In brief, the White House created a situation that drew more attention than needed because it failed to respect the agency of the press to rebel against propaganda, even though the images distributed were mundane.

Image control alters routine practices of the press

The modern forces of ideological media and online media converge with the Obama administration in limiting historical and routine practices of the press. The White House did not act in accordance with the press in jointly representing the interests of the public. The mainstream press provides routine coverage of the president as part of its watchdog function. The White House participates to contribute its part in the creation of images serving as illusions. This relationship between the White House and the press frequently depends on the creation of illusions to maintain legitimacy. As the White House provides credentials to the press for more interior coverage, the press, in return, provides proof that the president is engaged in presidential activities. Here structuration shows changes in a process, repeatedly, with the importance of symbolism. Image control allows the administration to align with historic images of Washington and Lincoln in the White House, as well as idealized depictions reminiscent of Kennedy in other settings (Frame, 2012) to create and reinforce ideas to the public.

The warm relationship between President George W. Bush's White House and Fox News created a ripple in the relationship between Obama and the press. Bush's image campaign was one that portrayed the apparent down-to-earth Texan as a masculine character who preferred to work on his ranch and who celebrated the military's initial victory over Iraq while this president was on a Navy ship. Bush's strength was the portrayal of confidence in the context of patriarchal masculinity. Obama's image campaign was a response to the inevitable negativity of Fox News. As a biracial Democrat, Obama could never play Bush's part in the theatre. His racial composite would always be a factor in the image he portrayed, so Obama's team appeared to minimize exposure. Because Fox News escalated its role in the system by rejecting the principle of American journalism objectivity while simultaneously suggesting it was its sole representative, the White House's role changed with the election of Obama. The response by Obama's White House was to alter its relationship with the press, and the White House had the power to do so as the leader of the Ideological State Apparatus.

Traditional images of power align with American expectations of the presidency

Obama, as the president, inherently embodies power, but he has difficulty representing it. In images, Obama operates within American symbolism crafted in traditional aspects of the office and portrayed through White House photographers in the Oval Office, larger meeting rooms, and neutral spaces. Efforts are taken to portray freedom, powerfulness or power sharing, and personality. Obama conveys the authenticity of the presidency but, at times, displays unease that is not aided through image control in different settings as seen in this work. In the images, power is displayed in setting, seating arrangements with others, and symbolic artifacts. However, traditional requirements of this job in a modern setting—such as dignitary dress and celebrity style—may mix uneasily as expectations of the U.S. president evolve for an American and global audience.

John Berger (1980) wrote of the comfort or discomfort of men in suits. "Almost anonymous as a uniform, it was the first ruling class costume to idealize purely sedentary power. The power of the administrator and conference table. Essentially the suit was made for the gestures of talking and calculating abstractly" (p. 38). Obama in a suit appears uncomfortable compared to his representations in images outside of formal meetings. He appears overly rigid in formal situations because that is exterior to his comfort zone. In contrast, Prince Charles appears more at ease in formal attire. The exclusion of photojournalists at specified meetings only draws attention to his representations—compared to Obama in a variety of conditions and under different representational frames—and associates him with some of the worst of his criticisms.

These displays may reflect an Obama strategy to manage image in light of race, arguably justified given press portrayals of his blackness (Holt, 2012). However, Obama has not challenged racist depictions from political opponents (Enck-Wanzer, 2011). From a system view, this lacking political or rhetorical challenge supports racial neoliberalism that undermines his administration. Obama's stance may result from being caught in the middle of critique for failing to be proactive on race versus risking "the charge of racism by violating the rhetorical norms of neoliberalism" or appearing different (Enck-Wanzer, 2011, p. 28). A mundane and presidential legitimacy conveyed in symbols and meanings limits the idea that this president strays from the norms of the nation's highest office and allows image management to lessen the impact of race.

Conclusion

The effectiveness of ideological management is possible through creating a make-believe reality. Not allowing photojournalists to cover particular events led to public revelation of photojournalists' exclusion, therefore creating awareness of an imposed ideology. Ironically, including photojournalists for mundane events would have provided the cover of a free and active press. The moments that will encourage people to take more critical examinations of the effects of government policies and elites' actions are those outside the White House—not in it. This work was limited to analysis of photographs released by the Obama administration because of the controversy the exclusions stirred with the administration and some media outlets. With new media channels, video offers another format for analysis. Expanded political and news context related to subjects in presidential photographs and videos would provide further exploratory insight.

Potentially, the Obama administration's efforts to limit press coverage may speak to a shift in state-imposed response to new media channels. Traditionally, the press corps fulfilled a watchdog and First Amendment role in monitoring, reporting, and interpreting the happenings of the White House. With special privilege and access, this group represented mainstream media institutions in covering the presidential bureaucracy. Yet the social media president has done well in cultivating a particular image despite varied performance that has not fared well with political adversaries. Therefore, the limit of access to photojournalists may have more to do with setting a stage for controlled representation; a test toward what could happen with limited access.

Further, the state of disparate new media channels coexisting with traditional media open the opportunity to justify limited access based on demographic shifts away from mass media. Regardless of motivation, limited access may aid the administration in crafting the desired image that speaks directly as an authentic brand to the American public without threatening their competency and using various channels that allow co-creation of presidential identity. Inherent in new media is two-way interaction that supports authenticity, reciprocity, and co-creation with audiences. What may seem mundane in terms of images could indeed signal the dramatic shift to a diminishing influence of the mainstream media in supporting the ISA—a restructuration of press agency that allows more direct ISA control and a reduction of the freedom of the press.

Notes

1. A copy of the letter can be found here: http://asne.org/blog_home.asp?Display=1649.

2. See http://www.nydailynews.com/news/politics/behind-the-scenes-president-obama-gallery-1.1232456?pmSlide=1.1232433; http://www.flickr.com/photos/whitehouse/9095096213/; http://www.flickr.com/photos/whitehouse/8735932090/

References

Althusser, L. (2014). *On the reproduction of capitalism: Ideology and ideological state apparatuses.* London, England: Verso Books.

Bang, H. (2009). "Yes we can": Identity politics and project politics for the late-modern world. *Urban Research and Practice, 2*(2), 1–21.

Banister, E. N., & Cocker, H. L. (2014). A cultural exploration of consumers' interactions and relationships with celebrities. *Journal of Marketing Management, 30*(1–2), 1–29.

Barrett, T. (2012). *Criticizing photographs: An introduction to understanding images.* New York, NY: McGraw-Hill.

Barthes, R. (1973). *Mythologies.* St. Albans, England: Paladin.

Bell, K. (2011). "A delicious way to help save lives": Race, commodification, and celebrity in product (RED). *Journal of International and Intercultural Communication, 4,* 163–180.

Berger, J. (1980). *About looking.* New York, NY: Vintage International.

Boorstin, D. J. (1962). *The image: A guide to pseudo-events in America.* New York, NY: Harper Colophone Books.

Bourdieu, P. (1991). *Language and symbolic power.* Cambridge, MA: Harvard University Press.

Bourdieu, P., Wacquant, L. J. D., & Farage, S. (1994). Rethinking the state: Genesis and structure of the bureaucratic field. *Sociological Theory, 12*(1), 1–18.

Couldry, N. (2003). *Media rituals: A critical approach.* New York, NY: Routledge.

De Chernatony, L. (1999). Brand management through narrowing the gap between brand identity and brand reputation. *Journal of Marketing Management, 15*(1–3), 157–179.

Enck-Wanzer, D. (2011). Barack Obama, the Tea Party, and the threat of race: On racial neoliberalism and born again racism. *Communication, Culture & Critique, 4*(1), 23–30.

Erickson, K. V. (2000, June). Presidential rhetoric's visual turn: Performance fragments and the politics of illusionism. *Communication Monographs, 67,* 138–157.

Frame, G. (2012). Seeing Obama, projecting Kennedy: The presence of JFK in images of Barack Obama. *Comparative American Studies, 10,* 163–176.

Garcia, A. (2012, May 29). Will citizen photojournalism take over the news industry? *Chicago Tribune Assignment Chicago Blog* [Online]. Retrieved from http://newsblogs.chicagotribune.com/assignment-chicago/2012/05/will-citizen-photojournalism-take-over-the-news-industry.html

Giddens, A. (1993). *The Giddens reader.* Stanford, CA: Stanford University Press.

Gleason, T. R. (2005). The candidate behind the curtain: A three-step program for analyzing campaign Issues. *SIMILE: Studies in Media & Information Literacy Education, 5.* Retrieved from https://www.academia.edu/15475955/The_Candidate_Behind_the_Curtain_A_Three-step_Program_for_Analyzing_Campaign_Images.

Hall, S. (1980). Encoding/decoding. In S. Hall, D. Hobson, A. Lowe, & P. Willis (Eds.), *Culture, media, language* (pp. 128–138). London, England: Hutchinson.

Hand, M. (2012). *Ubiquitous photography.* Cambridge, England: Polity Press.

Hariman, R., & Lucaites, J. L. (2007). *No caption needed: Iconic photographs, public culture, and liberal democracy.* Chicago, IL: The University of Chicago Press.

Holt, L. F. (2012). Hillary and Barack: Will atypical candidates lead to atypical coverage? *Howard Journal of Communications, 23,* 272–287.

den Hond, F., Boersma, F. K., Heres, L., Kroes, E. H., & van Oirschot, E. (2012). Giddens à la Carte? Appraising empirical applications of Structuration Theory in management and organization studies. *Journal of Political Power, 5,* 239–264.

Hope, D. S. (2006). Identity and visual communication. In D. S. Hope, *Visual communication: Perception, rhetoric, and technology* (pp. 5–27). Cresskill, NJ: Hampton Press, Inc.

Jenkins, H. (2006). *Convergence culture: Where old and new media collide*. New York, NY: New York University Press.

Kellner, D. (2009). Barack Obama and celebrity spectacle. *International Journal of Communication, 3*, 27.

Mac, A. (2012, Sept. 7). Social media insights inspired by Barack Obama, America's first truly social president. *Fast Company*. Retrieved from http://www.fastcompany.com/3001091/social-media-insights-inspired-barack-obama-americas-first-truly-social-president

Merrigan, G., & Huston, C. L. (2004). *Communication research methods*. Belmont, CA: Thomson.

Olson, L. C., Finnegan, C. A., & Hope, D. (2008). *Visual rhetoric: A reader in communication and American culture*. Thousand Oaks, CA: Sage Publications.

Peck, J. (1987). Interview. In N. Chomsky, *The Chomsky reader* (pp. 1–55). New York, NY: Pantheon Books.

Schiller, H. J. (1989). *Culture, Inc.: The corporate takeover of public expression*. New York, NY: Oxford University Press.

Shoemaker, P. J. (1991). *Gatekeeping*. Newbury Park, CA: Sage Publications.

Steinhauser, P. (2012, April 26). Web ad mocks Obama as 'celebrity president'. *CNN Politics*. Retrieved from http://politicalticker.blogs.cnn.com/2012/04/26/web-ad-mocks-obama-as-celebrity-president/

Stempel, G. H., III (1985). Gatekeeping: The mix of topics and the selection of stories. *Journalism Quarterly, 62*, 791–796, 815.

Sullivan, S. (2013, October 22). The end of lovable Obama? Maybe. *The Washington Post*. Retrieved from http://www.washingtonpost.com/blogs/the-fix/wp/2013/10/22/the-end-of-lovable-obama-maybe/

Thomson, M. (2006). Human brands: Investigating antecedents to consumers' strong attachments to celebrities. *Journal of Marketing, 70*, 104–119.

Tuchman, G. (1978). *Making news: A study in the construction of reality*. New York, NY: The Free Press.

"To Have Your Experience Denied … it Hurts": Barack Obama, James Baldwin, and the Politics of Black Anger[1]

Jeffrey B. Kurtz

ABSTRACT
This article argues that Barack Obama's rhetorical example–captured in 4 addresses in response to acts of violence–suggests habits of mind to help us begin to navigate perhaps the most vexing democratic conundrum of our age: Can we find words to realize reconciliation and trust across lines of racial difference, given the violence that infects our efforts to talk to each other? The tensions occasioned by the intersection of race and violence comprised the defining conditions of Obama's presidency. The underpinnings of those conditions and the ways Obama rhetorically worked within them invite us to profoundly rethink how we might articulate a nuanced civic honesty, an honesty inflected by the rhetorical-politics of Black anger modeled by James Baldwin. Together, this honesty, that anger, illuminate understandings of the ways Obama marshaled rhetorical resources to combat the political lynchings ravaging our contemporary civic polity.

"Now, I'm not naïve. I have spoken at too many memorials during the course of this presidency." —Barack Obama (2016)

"Here … in this nation, race and the future seem so intertwined as to be the same thing." —Lawrence Jackson (2016, p. 40)

"There are some things we should be angry about." —Viet Thanh Nguyen (qtd. in Kim, 2013, p. 178)

What if democracy foremost is about kinship? Barack Obama rightly will be remembered for his oratory, but it was perhaps his efforts to work through his own understandings of kinship—namely, his relationship to his father—that first signaled his was a voice richly sensitive to the trials of belonging, the odyssey demanded of memory, the joy and pain that flows from coming to terms with our fleeting innocence, and how much these feelings matter for our democracy (Obama, 1995).

Surely among Obama's inspirations for his provocative memoir was James Baldwin, who also grasped profoundly and unsentimentally the ways our most intimate (i.e., closest) relationships form the foundations on which we build our democratic strivings. This depth of Baldwin's thinking was a particularly moving display in "Notes of a Native Son," first published in 1955 as collection of essays with the same title. Among reasons why the essay was so striking was because Baldwin tacked between the deeply personal and the profoundly public to advance a blistering understanding of the relationship between race, anger, and democracy.

That essay opened with a familiar juxtaposition: the slim gap between life and death. On the one hand, Baldwin opened his chronicle by relating the death of his father, David, on July 29, 1943. Within hours of his passing, Baldwin's father's last child was born in Harlem. What was significant about Baldwin's leveraging of this juxtaposition was the context he put around it. He wrote,

> Over a month before this, while all our energies were concentrated in waiting for these events, there had been, in Detroit, one of the bloodiest race riots of the century. A few hours after my father's funeral, while he lay in state in the undertaker's chapel, a race riot broke out in Harlem. On the morning of the 3rd of August, we drove my father to the graveyard through a wilderness of smashed plate glass. The day of my father's funeral had also been my nineteenth birthday. As we drove him to the graveyard, the spoils of injustice, anarchy, discontent, and hatred were all around us. (Baldwin, 1998, p. 63)

This work of contextualization is familiar to students of rhetoric. What I want to impress is the relationship between the context upon which Baldwin builds his memories of his father's death and the matters of race, violence, and democratic injustice that seep across the introduction to the essay. What Baldwin established at the outset was the conviction that life and death, tragedy and joy, race and violence are all intertwined in a tapestry that achingly reveals, as Turner (2011) essayed, why "white supremacy [must be seen] as a form of mental and moral slumber" (p. 89).

White supremacy, moreover, functions in our contemporary moment to embolden what I term practices of *political lynching*, habits of speech and action that collectively, to borrow from Hendricks (2009), collude to facilitate our collective political death, a death prompted by the "prolonged [moral] torment and torture" of our democratic practices (p. 180).

Baldwin understood profoundly the risks of not talking back to the torment propagated by lynching's horrific violence; silence ensured both Blacks' erasure through extermination and whites' doom through anxious, endless guilt (Weisenburger, 2005, p. 5). This understanding, the sense of righteous civic anger that infused it, was something Obama grasped. Of foremost importance about Obama's rhetoric was its capacious civic and moral imagination and the ways that imagination reframed understandings of our democratic moment within the crucible of race and violence (Isaksen, 2011; Miller, 2013; Terrill, 2009). Working through four pivotal moments from that rhetorical corpus—the addresses after the shootings in Tucson, Newtown, and Charleston, and Obama's remarks following the not-guilty verdict of George Zimmerman for the murder of Trayvon Martin—this article strives to understand better the rhetorical inheritance Obama left us. That inheritance is comprised of trenchant gestures toward a Baldwinian civic honesty (1963), an honesty tinted by anger about the political lynchings taking place in our midst.

Over the remainder of this article, I work through the intellectual and moral consequences of Obama's texts as these played out against one of the most vexing political-democratic conundrums of our age: Can we find the words by which reconciliation and trust might be realized across lines of racial difference, given the violence that relentlessly infects our efforts to talk to each other? In Obama's public address we see the necessity of facing this conundrum squarely. Yet scholars also have noted the ways Obama's rhetorical discourse resists easy analysis. That resistance, as Bromell (2013) illuminated, stems in part from the ways Obama's "positions reflect his analysis of political realities, not his theory of democracy [more generally]" (p. 141). We also should recognize, as Sugrue (2010) did, that "Obama … captures the ambiguities of a racial order that denies racism yet is rife with racial inequality; that celebrates progress when celebration is not always warranted. He contains within his own thought contradictory positions that remain in tension with each other" (p. 136). In complement to Sugrue (2010), I will show the ways in which the tensions occasioned by the intersection of race and violence comprised the defining rhetorical conditions of Obama's presidency. These conditions invite us to profoundly rethink how we might articulate the commitments that comprise a more a nuanced civic honesty inflected by what Baldwin (1963, 1998) illustrated as a productive anger. The remainder of this article demonstrates the ways Obama creatively re-read violence to promote critical reflections about our shared lives together and rhetorically imagined "race" as a platform on which to build moral insights about the meanings of our democracy. These meanings suggest how we might channel collective anger toward richer civic ends and assume new vigilance against the political lynchings violating our civic deliberations. Olson's distinction (2011) is helpful here: "Characterized as merely personal, anger may be mis-recognized as a maladjusted individual, not as a malfunctioning culture that rational people out to experience with outrage" (p. 288). By weaving together these threads of civic anger, race, and violence, a new perspective on Obama's political discourse emerges.

Baldwinian outrage and political lynchings

One reason Obama's rhetorical performances were compelling for our democratic possibilities was due to the ways he channeled a Baldwinian anger in response to our "business-as-usual" reactions to the tragedies of racial/racist acrimony and gun violence. The nature of this anger has much to teach us. As Balfour (1999) uncovered, it was Baldwin's "aspiration" to marshal a language in service to a critique of racist injustice without "losing sight" for "the complicated workings of race consciousness in American society" (p. 75). At the core of this aspiration, as Bromell (2013) noted, was Baldwin's "especially keen awareness … that relationships and acts of recognition are often political activities with powerful implications for a democratic polity" (p. 59). Baldwin, in other words, penned essays that assisted "readers in uncovering the habits of thought and 'habits of the heart' that stymie or nurture democratic possibilities in light of the ongoing significance of race" (Balfour, 1999, p. 79). Out of these essays emerged an ethic of acceptance that signaled Baldwin's commitment to an "active opposition to innocence, [to] a confrontation with life's hardest truths" (Balfour, 1999, p. 89). This active opposition sometimes assumed strident tones:

> White man, hear me! History ... does not refer merely or even principally to the past. On the contrary, the great force of history comes from the fact that we carry within us, are unconsciously controlled by it in many ways, so history is literally present in all that we do. It could scarcely be otherwise since it is to history that we owe our frames of reference, our identities, and our aspirations. (Baldwin qtd. in Shulman, 2013, p. 149)

Baldwin's political thought demonstrated prophetic force and historical acumen, ways of thinking about how the past pulled on people's lives to inspire fear and how that fear compelled civic and moral cowardice. His moral power derived from the ways he injected an unapologetic sense of reality into his musings about one of the most glaring fault lines across the human condition: Our inability to confront our past and our present as regards matters of race (Glaude, 2016).

Obama should be judged a rightful inheritor of Baldwin's civic anger. That inheritance is best understood by echoing similarities Muyumba (2014) identified in his discussion of Baldwin and John Dewey: Like Dewey, Obama played the role of a cultural critic who, "through [his] own 'inventions and arrangements,' persuade[d] individuals to invent and arrange their experiences expansively" (p. 161). Obama's anger should be recognized not as expressions of rage for the sake of rage, but, like Baldwin, for the ways that that anger—and particularly its discursive dimensions—reconstituted our civic polity into "a reticulate public sphere wherein analyses of their [African American] impressions and their subsequent expression generate[d] knowledge" (Muyumba, 2014, p. 169). At the core of this anger Obama modeled was, *qua* Baldwin, "an unshakeable human authority" that challenged citizens to wrestle with the opportunities found in reconciliation (Muyumba, 2014, p. 169). This potential for reconciliation, however, was profoundly burdened by the specter of political lynchings that hovered over the president's rhetorical performances.

In offering the term *political lynchings*, I mean not to parrot the vernacular politicians bandy about in response to unfair treatment. Nor am I gesturing disrespectfully to the United States' brutal history of lynching (Dray, 2002). Instead, I am thinking of political lynchings principally as a metaphor to lend theoretical cachet to arguments about Obama's rhetorical legacy. Echoing the historical analysis of Wood (2009), I want to suggest that political lynchings hinge upon a culture of spectacle. As she observed, "To understand lynching in relationship to ... spectacle is not only to comprehend the excess and horrifying cruelty of lynching but also to make sense of the impulse that compelled so many people to look at scenes of torture and suffering with eagerness and approval" (Wood, 2009, p. 3). In working with the idea of political lynchings, I want to impress that Obama's rhetorical corpus—the selective corpus considered here—suggests how spectacle has corrupted our civic relationships to one other. These tensions have configured themselves in such rhetorical habits as an indifference to history and a capitulation to hate, ignorance, and rudeness that together make it almost impossible to reclaim a sense of democratic integrity from the spectacle of political lynching run amok (Greenfield, 2016).[2] In the texts considered here we see how Obama pushed to re-establish the relevance of history and the necessary application of such rhetorical habits as civic honesty, compassion, and resilience in the aftermath of horrible violence. For the moment, however, I defer matters of analysis to reflect on the responses of some of Obama's most vocal critics.

Obama and his critics

A variety of voices registered discontent with the president's tenure. A political columnist bemoaned "two versions of President Barack Obama: one who preaches unity, compromise, listening to opponents and avoiding division, and one who, in practice, doesn't compromise, doesn't listen, spouts nastiness and alienates" (Ambrose, 2016, p. B11). Other critics registered frustration over the president's lack of prophetic leadership (West, 2014), rhetorical impotence (Coates, 2012), historical amnesia (Cobb, 2010), policy diffidence (Bonilla-Silva, 2014), racial timidity (Dyson, 2016), and democratic cowardice (Ikard & Teasley, 2012; Glaude, 2016). Coates remarked on the irony of Barack Obama becoming "the most successful Black politician in America history by avoiding the radioactive racial issues of yesteryear." Ikard and Teasley (2012) maintained that Obama's skirting of "racism and colorism ... trivialize[d] the unique and underpublicized cost of being black in America" (p. 54). Glaude (2016) chastised the president for selling "black America the snake oil of hope and change" (p. 7). Perhaps Obama's most outspoken critic, West (2014) bemoaned that the defining themes for black America during the "age of Obama" were "desperation, confusion, and capitulation" (p. 163).

Terrill (2015) encapsulated well the tenor of these criticisms, noting the ways "critics and observers have argued that Obama succumbed to the limitations of this bargain [i.e., by electing a Black president the United States had overcome racism] and as a result has not addressed race directly in any very satisfactorily transformative manner" (p. 152). Yet I believe Shulman (2008) was correct: In simply participating in the long historical conversation about forms of racial domination, Obama productively showcased the "rhetorical and political difficulties in addressing them" (p. xvii). The rhetorical challenges of transformation cannot be overstated; such efforts will remain extraordinarily difficult. As Terrill (2015) remarked, Obama presented a paradoxical—and helpful—picture of the rhetorical habits our civic polity requires to realize the atonement missing from contemporary gestures toward reconciliation; the "remarkable thing about Obama's discourse," Terrill reflected, was "not how little it explicitly confronts issues of race but how thoroughly it addresses so many issues through an idiom rooted in race" (p. 152). Or as Hatch (2009) remarked, "For race relations, as for Obama, the way forward appears to lie in a rhetorical enlargement of liberation encompassing both individual and collective histories, identities, rights, power, and well-being—through discourse that interweaves the personal and the public" (pp. 487–488). More precisely, the way forward Obama modeled was to articulate a productive civic anger. The rhetorical dimensions of that anger, echoing Marshall's insight (2011) about Baldwin, constituted "an expression of American democratic virtue, as a form of the distinctive excellence of a democratic citizen" (p. 192). This virtue the president modeled was all the more remarkable as it unfolded within a culture of seemingly relentless violence.

Violence, rhetoric, and our civic polity

Violence is difficult to conceptualize as a critical/rhetorical heuristic. As Warner (2003) recognized, "to classify ... violence already is to stand outside [it]" (p. 44). What, then, is at stake for thinkers, writers, speakers, and activists who insist upon using violence as a source for rhetorical invention and moral reflection? Volger and Markell (2003) asked a similar question: "To survive violence, to find a way forward under its weight: Is this less or more radical than to dream of overcoming violence in a final, exceptional stroke?" (p. 3). Browne (1999), locating in the rhetorical example of the nineteenth-century abolitionist Angelina Grimke a peculiar commitment "to make of herself 'an available means of persuasion,'" demonstrated how she courageously "transform[ed] violence into a catalyst for social change" (p. 11); that is, Grimke showed how "what might be viewed as a check on social change— violence—is rhetorically transformed into a specific and highly charged rationale for collective action" (p. 11). Most recently, Engels (2015) articulated a set of critical commitments wherein the "critique of violence is [seen as] inherent to social order"; the "critique of violence refuses to mark violence as *exceptional*" (p. 119; italics added for emphasis). Obama's rhetorical examples illuminated ways violence and race may serve collective moral ends. These ends pointed toward distinctly new ways of seeing and understanding our civic obligations to one another. Gesturing once more to Engels (2015): "It matters how we address our friends and enemies.... Violence is the product of a rhetorical culture that has embraced the politics of resentment" (p. 152). If Obama did not (could not?) placate our resentment, he demonstrated a compelling set of rhetorical practices whereby we see how talking about race and violence in keys of productive anger foreshadow potential opportunities for democratic healing.

How to explain the shootings in Tucson, Newton, and Charleston? What words could convey the disappointment of the Zimmerman verdict? Obama's moral task was to find words to work through the violence at the center of these events; in fact, it was within the crucible of violence that Obama named a redemptive pattern of political and moral thought. This pattern was inflected by Scripture, but more significant was the demonstration of a rhetorical imagination through which he argued for possibilities of redemption, renewal, and civic resilience. Frank (2014) candidly assessed the speeches Obama delivered after Tucson and Sandy Hook. Those speeches articulated "ways we might cope with the death of innocents resulting from gun violence" and more broadly set down distinct responses to evil (Frank, 2014, p. 654). Although part of the genre of rhetorical discourse characterized as epideictic (speeches aligned to offer comfort and consolation to a wider community), the speeches differed in "their theological, rhetorical, and policy aspirations" (Frank, 2014, p. 653). Frank's readings of these addresses showed keen attention to the differing theological assumptions Obama plied across each speech. Not fully appreciated, however, was the civic honesty in both texts. This honesty was not merely Obama's recognition that we face more forthrightly, as he spoke in Tucson, the obligation incumbent upon "all Americans," to understand that "we can question each other's ideas without questioning each other's love of country and that our task, working together, is to constantly widen the circle of our concern" (2011). Both addresses also articulated the need for a daring civility characterized by moral courage, intellectual vulnerability, and regard for the common good.

Within the textual dynamics of the Tucson address, in particular, this civic honesty showed itself in a rhetorical pivot with the roll call of those killed in the shooting. Mentioned last was 9-year-old Christina Taylor Green. The death of innocence and possibility modeled in Christina's life infused the text with a compelling stasis: We were rendered mute by the horror of the tragedy; a child is dead. Yet the president did not wallow in the maudlin. Instead, he reminded us that Christina's murder was one of six and that the collective pain of this tragedy crossed any and all divisions. In grief was an opportunity through which to realize that "our hearts have reason for fullness" (Obama, 2011). That fullness, however, was not confined to sentimentality; the text asked considerably more.

Foremost among the speech's solicitations was to make meaning from the horrible tragedy. Creating and establishing those meanings, however, was tied to the trenchant civic honesty that drove the rhetorical action of the text. This honesty, that anger showed itself when the president remarked, "You see, when a tragedy like this strikes, it is part of our nature to demand explanations—to try to impose some order on the chaos, and make sense out of that which seems senseless" (Obama, 2011). What was distinct here was the recognition about the unpredictability of our shared lives. And although we may, as the president acknowledged, take up threads of conversation concerned with the alleged shooter's motives or the soundness of gun safety laws or the inadequacy of our mental health systems, those conversations, the desire for control they belie, are not enough. Rational explanations neither will comfort nor redeem us. Something else was needed. Required was a rhetorical vulnerability precipitated by honest recognition that we have shared obligations to one another, obligations sustained by gestures of genuine reflection and the values of generosity and tempered heroism which may follow. Resources for such generosity and reflection may be found across the discursive landscape; the president posited Scripture as one source to conceptualize the rhetorical vulnerability we require. As he remarked, "In the words of Job, 'when I look for light, then came darkness.' Bad things happen, and we must guard against simple explanations in the aftermath" (Obama, 2011).

If the Tucson address turned principally on the roll call of the victims, a different pivot characterized the Sandy Hook speech. That pivot materialized when Obama, after rehearsing the tragedy of the mass shooting and celebrating the teachers, first responders, and students who demonstrated examples of "strength and resolve and sacrifice" (Obama, 2012), gestured to an uncomfortable fact: If Newtown had shown profound compassion and love in the face of "unconscionable evil," the tragedy left our nation with "some hard questions" (p. 3). Likening those questions to the paradoxical joy and anxiety of parenthood—like "having your heart outside your body all the time, walking around"—the president insisted that a society's "first task," "our first job" was to care for all children; if we failed to "get that right, we don't get anything right. That's how, as a society, we will be judged" (Obama, 2012). This judgment rested upon deceptively simple questions that merit quoting at length:

> Can we truly say, as a nation, that we are meeting our obligations? Can we honestly say that we're doing enough to keep our children—all of them—safe from harm? Can we claim, as a nation, that we're all together there, letting them know that they are loved, and teaching them to love in return? Can we say that we're truly doing enough to give all the children of this country the chance they deserve to live out their lives with happiness and with purpose? (Obama, 2012)

In their pointed civic honesty, these questions gestured to a higher plane of citizenship, one on which the fundamental tenet of our shared civic lives is to reject violence and especially the myriad, insidious ways violence can rend community.

The spirit and practice of reflection prompted by these questions underscored, moreover, the sense of urgency that inflects the moral and political obligations we have to reject violence. That rejection only will be realized by enacting fundamental habits of mind: genuine civic honesty, uncompromising reflection, and gestures to a necessary public anger. This, then, is why the crucible of violence presents such a useful heuristic to work through Obama's rhetorical legacy: Violence is akin to the air we breathe. And because we must breathe to live, the work of our shared civic lives is to find ways to reimagine and reclaim from violence a greater sense of moral efficacy. This efficacy requires we contextualize and foreground violence within the crucible of race, something Obama well-understood, as may be seen in his remarks after the George Zimmerman verdict and mass murder in Charleston, South Carolina.

Race and acknowledgment

On July 19, 2013 the president gave a press conference. By itself, this act was not unusual. What was remarkable was the subject of those remarks: an explicit reflection on the George Zimmerman verdict, announced the day before. On trial for the murder of 17-year-old Trayvon Martin, Zimmerman had been found not guilty. The verdict set off a maelstrom of cultural and social commentary. Lost in the maelstrom was a substantive consideration of what Obama actually said during his press conference, and especially the questions implied by his impromptu reflections: How should we think about the legacy of racist violence that mars our shared democratic experience? What might it mean to take seriously the primacy of experience when considering the meanings of the Zimmerman verdict? Above all, Obama recognized that context mattered to our efforts at collective interpretation and deliberation. He turned fully into that recognition, noting, "I did want to talk just a little bit about context and how people have responded to it [the verdict] and how people are feeling" (Obama, 2013).

The verdict and its aftermath posed intense challenges to our nation's faith in (imperfect) equal justice. That faith, especially among African Americans, suffered profound testing in the wake of the Zimmerman verdict. As Obama (2013) remarked,

> And when you think about why, in the African-American community at least, there's a lot of pain around what happened here, I think it's important to recognize that the African-American community is looking at these issues through a set of experiences and a history that—that doesn't go away .... And you know, I don't want to exaggerate this, but those sets of experiences inform how the African-American community interprets what happened one night in Florida. And it's inescapable for people to bring those experiences to bear.

What Obama did with this gesture to context was underscore that laws and judicial proceedings do not unfold in cultural or historical vacuums. More fundamentally, the gesture reflected a moral sensibility, an insistence on acknowledging that rational deliberation and its cousins of disinterest and objectivity function to perpetuate a kind of violence, violence predicated on forgetting and indifference to the pain caused by political lynching. That lynching not only constitutes egregious loss—of acknowledgment, of dignity—but also spurs the collective pain that follows from the profound dismissal of experience.

That pain and suffering, importantly, did not stand for Obama as an endpoint. Instead, the endpoint was the courageous imagining of civic deliberations inflected by moral courage and reflective compassion. Yet these qualities could not be abstracted from a sense of (civic, moral, personal) loss and a corresponding anger. It was Obama's insistence on the centrality of loss that seemed especially paramount during the press conference. With loss surely comes frustration and pain, yet Obama was not content to reside there. He recognized how intertwined were violence and race to our articulations about democracy (Glaude, 2016), noting:

> We understand that some of the violence that takes place in poor black neighborhoods around the country is born out of a very violent past in this country, and that the poverty and dysfunction that we see in those communities can be traced to a very difficult history. And so the fact that sometimes that's unacknowledged adds to the frustration. (Obama, 2013)

Acknowledgment matters so profoundly.

Rhetoric, anger, and hope

Obama's presidency was defined within the crucible of violence and race. Perhaps no incident more graphically portrayed that crucible than the mass shooting at Mother Emanuel Church in Charleston, South Carolina in June 2015. That shooting, which resulted in the murder of nine African Americans, signified the ways guns and (racial) difference had become the most polarizing issues of our contemporary moment. In eulogizing South Carolina state senator Reverend Clementa Pinckney, Obama renounced the political lynchings that had become so prevalent in early twenty-first century American political culture; his address was a provocative example of Baldwinian anger "talking back" to the attack on democracy represented in the horrific shooting (hooks, 1989).

Obama used the rhetorical-moral platform at Charleston's Mother Emanuel Church to argue for the salience of historical perspective and to underscore political habits of mind with which we might navigate our way through the horrific crucible that spurred the murder of the Charleston Nine. That perspective, those habits, may be encapsulated this way: As terrible as the violence that marred Charleston's most historic African American church was, it was in fact the history out of which the church emerged, the meanings of that history, which could serve as a salvo for healing, unity, and the critical reflection democracy requires.

The president complemented his profoundly moving eulogy to Pinckney with a different register, one that emphasized the significance of the Black church in American history and especially for African Americans. Invoking that history served two aims. First, Obama reinforced the inescapable racial tincture of the shooting—all of the murdered were African Americans, the killer White. Yet central to that tincture also was the fact that the horrific murder took place in a church, and the centrality of the church to the lives of African Americans could not be overstated. As Obama (2015) underscored, "The church is and always has been the center of African-American life—a place to call our own in a too often hostile world, a sanctuary from so many hardships." The text painted the church not merely as a gathering place for worship, but as a harbor where African Americans gathered in safety to sing songs of religious praise and recognize and cultivate the necessary seeds of resistance against White supremacy. This ethic of resistance is one of the hallmarks of African American culture. Here was how Obama (2015) used that history:

> Over the course of centuries, black churches served as "hush harbors" where slaves could worship in safety; praise houses where their free descendants could gather and shout hallelujah; rest stops for the weary along the Underground Railroad; bunkers for the foot soldiers of the Civil Rights Movement. They have been, and continue to be, community centers where we organize for jobs and justice; places of scholarship and network; places where children are loved and fed and kept out of harm's way, and told that they are beautiful and smart and taught that they matter. That's what happens in church.

This description was not merely a historical catalogue; central to the description also was a moral argument: The church, properly understood, was and continues to be a beacon and a bunker; a landmark by which African Americans safely navigated the terrors of White supremacy and within its walls created conditions of agency and resistance and empowerment.

If the racial cast of the shooting, and the historical context within and around it, was important for the president to reinforce, immersion in the historical legacy of the church served a second aim. In invoking this legacy, Obama stretched it toward universal ends, ends encompassed in the binds of trust, compassion, and political courage that should unite citizens of goodwill. These ties depend not on shared faith convictions but on shared convictions rooted in universal values. Those values, as the president sketched, were ones that both resisted White supremacy and fortified the practices of democracy. Again, Obama (2015) said,

> Often there were laws banning all-black church gatherings, services happened here anyway, in defiance of unjust laws. When there was a righteous movement to dismantle Jim Crow, Dr. Martin Luther King, Jr., preached from its pulpit, and marches began from its steps. A sacred place, this church. Not just for blacks, not just for Christians, but for every American who cares about the steady expansion of human rights and human dignity in this county; a foundation stone for liberty and justice for all. That's what the church [has] meant.

As he had done in Tucson and Newtown, the president marshalled key rhetorical resources—namely, an expansive view of history coupled with the language of Christian faith—to press Charleston residents—and, really, the entire nation—not to succumb to the pall of violence. In memorializing the life and legacy of the Reverend Pinckney, the president articulated fundamental habits of mind that might resist the violence that had claimed innocent lives.

These habits were given the force of conviction through the text's appropriation of Pinckney's legacy—the moral and political examples that infused this legacy stood as a synecdoche that embodied how citizens must think about and relate to one another. Acknowledging the sheer uphill climb represented by trying to reform current firearm legislation, for example, the president insisted that resignation—giving up and giving into to a political and moral culture suffering from the infections of prejudice and rage and ennui that have sickened the body politic—was not an option; to do so would forsake the subject of the eulogy: "It would be a betrayal of everything Reverend Pinckney stood, I believe, if we allowed ourselves to slip into a comfortable silence again," the president stated. Moreover,

> once the eulogies have been delivered, once the TV cameras move on, to go back to business as usual—that's what we so often do to avoid uncomfortable truths about the prejudice that still infects our society. To settle for symbolic gestures without following up with the hard work of more lasting change—that's how we lose our way again. (Obama, 2015)

New habits were required; those habits gestured directly to the ways our contemporary civic lives may be reclaimed in the name of genuine democratic recognition. Required was a "deep appreciation for each other's history," the president argued (2015), borrowing Reverend Pinckney's words. We must cultivate deeper, more refined, and more honest "recognition of ourselves in each other" (Obama, 2015).

Drawing toward the conclusion of the eulogy, the president reflected on the time he has spent among mourners in Charleston:

> That's what I've felt this week—an open heart. That, more than any particular policy or analysis, is what's called upon right now, I think—what a friend of mine, the writer Marilynne Robinson calls "that reservoir of goodness, beyond, and of another kind, that we are able to do each other in the ordinary cause of things." (Obama, 2015)

This allusion to Robinson's "reservoir of goodness" should not be casually dismissed. What Obama realized in his eulogy really was nothing short of remarkable: The intertwining of history and civic lament and righteous anger, complemented by profound gratitude for the legacy of a man who had served so gallantly in both the arenas of faith and politics. What we have is an example of unapologetic civic recognition at once brutally honest and redemptive in its cast: We are, all of us, responsible to the murder of the Charleston Nine, for what died that day not only were wholly innocent victims; our democracy was lynched as well. Obama spoke angrily and with courage from a pulpit of esteemed privilege; that speech concerned itself, borrowing from Olson (2011), with demanding that those of us "of relatively privileged positions" center our democratic thinking more fully on the "lives and perspectives of marginalized groups" different from us (p. 301). In Charleston, the president had declared, simply and profoundly: We must remember, and we must never cease working.

Coda: On anger and democratic healing

I have sought in this article to craft a framework in which to think carefully about Obama's rhetorical legacy. That framework attempted to take seriously how the crucible of violence and race must be acknowledged as the defining rhetorical conditions in which the president thought through and articulated intellectual-moral-civic convictions that challenged our political complacency and resisted what I've characterized here as unabashed political lynchings of our shared civic obligations to one another. This, then, is why Obama matters: Like Baldwin, Obama's rhetorical discourse insisted that we acknowledge, strive to recover, and live into a kind of democratic faith. This faith confronted the world as it was, and argued, trenchantly, tirelessly, and with unshakeable conviction, for a world that might yet be. What Obama modeled was a good-faith effort to practice genuine arguments that flowed both from his mind and his heart; a commitment to enact and sustain discourses infused with honesty and love; and ways of speaking, finally, that never cowered from difference or shirked the moral responsibility to enact something akin to a civic bravery, a bravery emboldened by righteous Black anger. These rhetorical commitments asked everything of him. Scholars will continue to debate just how profoundly we will miss Obama's example. So too will citizens (Brooks, 2016).

Notes

1. See Obama (2016).
2. Greenfield (2016) did not use the term *political lynchings*, yet his article, with its emphases upon understanding better the ways one political party virulently delegitimizes another party's very capacity to govern embodies what I have in mind in using the metaphor as it concerns our civic polity.

References

Ambrose, J. (2016, June 1). The president should listen to his own speeches. *Columbus Dispatch*, p. B11.
Baldwin, J. (1963). *The fire next time*. New York, NY: The Dial Press.
Baldwin, J. (1998). Notes of a native son. In T. Morrison (Ed.), *Baldwin: collected essays* (pp. 63–85). New York, NY: The library of America.

Balfour, L. (1999). Finding the words: Baldwin, race consciousness and democratic theory. In D. McBride (Ed.), *James Baldwin now* (pp. 75–102). New York, NY: New York University Press.

Bonilla-Silva, E. (2014). *Racism without racists: Color-blind racism and the persistence of racial inequality in America* (4th ed.). Lanham, MD: Rowman & Littlefield Publishers, Inc.

Bromell, N. (2013). *The time is always now: Black thought and the transformation of US democracy.* New York, NY: Oxford University Press.

Browne, S. H. (1999). *Angelina Grimke: Rhetoric, identity, and the radical imagination.* East Lansing, MI: Michigan State University Press.

Brooks, D. (2016, February 9). I miss Barack Obama. *New York Times.* Retrieved from http://www.nytimes.com/2016/02/09/opinion/i-miss-barack-obama

Coates, T. (2012). Fear of a black president. *The Atlantic.* Retrieved from http://www.theatlantic.com/magazine/archive/2012/09/fear-of-a-black-president/309064/

Cobb, W. J. (2010). *The substance of hope: Barack Obama and the paradox of progress.* New York, NY: Walker and Company.

Dray, P. (2002). *At the hands of persons unknown: The lynching of black America.* New York, NY: Random House.

Dyson, M. E. (2016). *The Black presidency: Barack Obama and the politics of race in America.* Boston, MA: Houghton Mifflin Harcourt.

Engels, J. (2015). *The politics of resentment: A genealogy.* University Park, PA: Pennsylvania State University Press.

Frank, D. A. (2014). Facing Moloch: Barack Obama's national eulogies and gun violence. *Rhetoric and Public Affairs, 17,* 653–678.

Glaude, E.S. (2016). *Democracy in black: How race still enslaves the American soul.* New York, NY: Crown Publishers.

Greenfield, J. (2016, August 18). Why the GOP will never accept president Hillary Clinton. *Politico.* Retrieved from http://www.politico.com/magazine/story/2016/08/2016-gop-hillary-clinton-delegitimizing-dems-214170

Hatch, J. B. (2009). Dialogic rhetoric in letters across the divide: A dance of (good) faith toward racial reconciliation. *Rhetoric & Public Affairs, 12,* 485–532.

Hendricks, O. M. (2009). A more perfect (high-tech) lynching: Obama, the press, and Jeremiah Wright. In T. Denean Sharpley-Whiting (Ed.), *The speech: Race and Barack Obama's "A More Perfect Union"* (pp. 155–183). New York, NY: Bloomsbury.

Hooks, B. (1989). *Talking back: Thinking feminist, thinking black.* Boston, MA: South End Press.

Ikard, D., & Teasley, M. L. (2012). *Nation of cowards: Black activism in Barack Obama's post-racial America.* Bloomington, IN: Indiana University Press.

Isaksen, J. L. (2011). Obama's rhetorical shift: Insights for communication studies. *Communication Studies, 62,* 456–471.

Jackson, L. (2016, July). Letter from Baltimore: The city that bleeds; Freddie Gray and the makings of an American uprising. *Harper's,* pp. 40–47.

Kim, S. J. (2013). *On anger: Race, cognition, narrative.* Austin, TX: University of Texas Press.

Marshall, S. H. (2011). *The city on the hill from below: The crisis of prophetic Black politics.* Philadelphia, PA: Temple University Press.

Miller, J. C. (2013). From the parlor to the barnyard: Obama and Holder on race. *Communication Quarterly, 61,* 349–373.

Muyumba, W. (2014). All safety is an illusion: John Dewey, James Baldwin, and the democratic practice of pubic critique. In B. Jackson & G. Clark (Eds.), *Trained capacities: John Dewey, rhetoric, and democratic practice* (pp. 159–176). Columbia, SC: University of South Carolina Press.

Obama, B. (1995). *Dreams from my father: A story of race and inheritance.* New York, NY: Three Rivers Press.

Obama, B. (2011). *Remarks by the president at a memorial service for the victims of the shooting in Tucson, Arizona.* Retrieved from https://www.whitehouse.gov/the-press-office/2011/01/12/remarks-president-barack-obama-memorial-service-victims-shooting-tucson

Obama, B. (2012). *Remarks by the president at the Sandy Hook Interfaith Vigil.* Retrieved from https://www.whitehouse.gov/the-press-office/2012/12/16/remarks-president-sandy-hook-interfaith-prayer-vigil

Obama, B. (2013). *Remarks by the president on Trayvon Martin.* Retrieved from https://www.whitehouse.gov/the-press-office/2013/07/19/remarks-president-trayvon-martin

Obama, B. (2015). *Remarks by the president in eulogy for the Honorable Reverend Clementa Pinckney.* Retrieved from https://www.whitehouse.gov/the-press-office/2015/06/26/remarks-president-eulogy-honorable-reverend-clementa-pinckney

Obama, B. (2016). *Remarks by the president at memorial service for fall Dallas police officers.* Retrieved from https://www.whitehouse.gov/the-press-office/2015/06/26/remarks-president-eulogy-honorable-reverend-clementa-pinckney

Olson, L. C. (2011). Anger among allies: Audre Lorde's 1981 keynote admonishing the National Women's Studies Association. *Quarterly Journal of Speech, 97,* 283–308.

Shulman, G. (2008). *American prophecy: Race and redemption in American political culture.* Minneapolis, MN: University of Minnesota Press.

Sugrue, T. J. (2010). *Not even past: Barack Obama and the burden of race.* Princeton, NJ: Princeton University Press.

Terrill, R. E. (2009). Unity and duality in Barack Obama's "A more perfect union". *Quarterly Journal of Speech, 95,* 363–386.

Terrill, R. E. (2015). *Double-consciousness and the rhetoric of Barack Obama: The price and promise of citizenship.* Columbia, SC: University of South Carolina Press.

Turner, J. (2011). *Awakening to race: individualism and social consciousness in America.* Chicago, IL: University of Chicago Press.

Vogler, C., & Markell, P. (2003). Introduction: Violence, redemption, and the liberal imagination. *Public Culture, 15,* 1–10.

Warner, M. (2003). What like a bullet can undeceive? *Public Culture, 15,* 41–54.

Weisenburger, S. (2002). The shudder and the silence: James Baldwin on white terror. *ANQ: A Quarterly Journal of Short Articles, Notes and Reviews, 15*(3), 3–12.

West, C. (2014). *Black prophetic fire.* Boston, MA: Beacon Press.

Wood, A. L. (2009). *Lynching and spectacle: witnessing racial violence in America, 1890–1940.* Chapel Hill, NC: University of North Carolina Press.

News Framing of Obama, Racialized Scrutiny, and Symbolic Racism

Srividya Ramasubramanian and Amanda R. Martinez

ABSTRACT
The current study examines the Barack Obama presidency through the lens of racialized news framing and symbolic racism. Racial prejudice often manifests as subtle symbolic racism in so-called postracial America by supporting beliefs that racial minorities have gained undeserved advantage and are no longer discriminated against. Even when counter-stereotypic leaders such as President Obama from racial/ethnic minority groups are elected to positions of authority, they are subject to tokenism, heightened visibility, and racialized scrutiny in the media in ways that reinforce cultural stereotypes. The current study uses a between-participants experiment ($N = 168$) to examine how exposure to positive versus negative news frames of Obama have differential effects on White participants' symbolic racist beliefs. From a priming perspective, exposure to negative frames of President Obama is likely to activate underlying prejudicial feelings that lead to biased evaluations of African Americans as a whole. Using path analysis, the present study builds a causal chain of relationships that reveals that exposure to negative news frames of Obama as compared to positive ones activates readers' anti-Black affect, which in turn increases their symbolic racist beliefs. Implications of the findings for race/ethnic studies, political communication and journalism are discussed.

The year 2008 marked an extraordinary moment in U.S. history when Barack Obama was elected as the nation's first African American president. The primary elections received unprecedented media coverage. News coverage analyses depicted Obama as educated, eloquent, and charismatic (Aronson, Jannone, McGlone, & Johnson-Campbell, 2009; Plant et al., 2009). This positive image was notably different from commonly held negative portrayals of Blacks in media as aggressive, unmotivated, and unintelligent (Bogle, 2001; Dixon, 2005; Entman & Rojecki, 2000). However, coverage of Obama by the mainstream media has also drawn on cultural stereotypes to cast him in a negative light. We argue that media framing of Obama shapes audiences' attitudes in subtle ways that reinforce symbolic racist beliefs that discrimination is no longer a concern and that racial/minorities are being too pushy for their political rights in so-called postracial contemporary American society.

Obama serves as a unique case study in media framing due to his complex intersectional identities unlike any American president in history. Logan (2011) asserted that common media frames of Obama simultaneously depict him as relatable to Black and White Americans by accentuating his distinctly Black male racialization yet neutralizing his differences by presenting him as the "guy next door" who strongly exemplifies White, American values. Compared to negative stereotypes of African Americans in media, Obama's multiculturalism, and Blackness in particular, is unthreatening: He holds a position of power, prestige, and authority; he is not angry, does not discuss racial grievances, and speaks of the goodness of the country and its diverse citizens (Logan, 2011; Richeson & Bean, 2011; Tesler & Sears, 2010). At times, he embodies a commitment to diversity by not shying away from race and multiculturalism issues in the United States.

Public figures from underrepresented groups often tread a delicate psychological tightrope in how media stories frame them. Although these media celebrities are sometimes framed positively as counter-stereotypic exemplars, these positive frames can quickly turn negative, especially during crisis situations. This study explores the effects of news frames of President Obama within the framework of symbolic racism, tokenism, and racialized scrutiny. Even when leaders from minority groups are appointed to powerful positions of authority, they are subject to heightened scrutiny and held to higher expectations than their counterparts from majority groups (Jackson, Thoits, & Taylor, 1995; Kanter, 1977; Wingfield & Wingfield, 2014).

Within this broader context of media's portrayals of leaders from minority groups, this study explores the differential effects of positive versus negative frames of President Obama in influencing White audiences' racial attitudes toward African Americans. Using an experimental design, we examine how news framing of Obama in positive ways as a successful leader or in negative ways as an unsuccessful leader affects readers' generalized appraisal of African Americans by activating prejudicial feelings, reinforcing stereotypical perceptions, and increasing symbolic racist beliefs. Furthermore, it tests the mediating role of anti-Black affect and negative stereotypical perceptions of African Americans in understanding the relationship between news exposure and symbolic racist attitudes.

Media celebrities, framing, and racial minorities

Media use a variety of strategies to frame and make salient particular schemas of public figures (Scheufele, 1999). Content analyses document that racial/ethnic minority groups are underrepresented, marginalized, and demeaned in mainstream media. For instance, African Americans are overrepresented as violent, criminal, and unmotivated in news, entertainment, and popular culture (Bogle, 2001; Dixon

& Linz, 2000; Entman & Rojecki, 2000; Mastro, 2000). The intergroup identity characteristics and contexts that impact whether, how, and to what extent audiences perceive and identify favorably with racially diverse media personalities remain complex and difficult to systematically explore (Plant et al., 2009; Schmidt & Nosek, 2010).

Prior studies assert that White audience members express more liking and social attraction to Black media celebrities when they approximate prototypically White in-group attributes, are highly assimilated, and participate in interracially harmonious interactions; these highly assimilated portrayals of Black out-group media celebrities exhibiting prized White in-group attributes (i.e., intelligence) affirm White audience members' self-concept as not racist (Coover, 2001; Mastro, Tamborini, & Hullett, 2005). Cashmore (2012) argued that White guilt anchors this process of dissociating and distancing from the undercurrents of the country's shameful race relations history. Logan (2011) asserted that White Americans may feel a sense of exemption from responsibility in dealing with race issues through such displays of inclusivity and liking but cautions that these are surface-level nods under the guise of antiracist action. Due to the fact that racial categorization remains foundational to the United States, many argue that Americans (particularly White Americans) cannot truly be colorblind because racial categories are automatically activated to some extent (Dovidio, Gaertner, Saguy, & Hehman, 2011).

Racialized imagery in the media need not include explicit negative stereotypes to bring about attitudinal changes. From a priming perspective, even subtle frames and implicit media cues can affect audiences' racial opinions and evaluations (Brown Givens, & Monahan, 2005; Ford, 1997; Ramasubramanian, 2011; Valentino, 1999). For instance, Ramasubramanian (2011) demonstrated that participants primed with images of stereotypical Black media celebrities compared to counter-stereotypical images reported higher negative feelings and real-world stereotypical perceptions of African Americans, which in turn decreased support for affirmative action. Similarly, Abraham and Appiah (2006) found that even when presented with news stories void of race mentions, White participants seemingly relied upon cultural stereotypes as sense-making schemas to understand race-based public policy issues.

Racial ambivalence, the myth of the American Dream, and symbolic racism

In examining the racial beliefs and attitudes of White Americans in the contemporary United States, overt forms of racism and prejudice toward specific target groups are generally not considered acceptable; instead, race neutrality and colorblindness persist (Sears & Henry, 2005). Considering that racism is increasingly expressed and experienced in subtle, nuanced, and aversive ways, symbolic racism measures are invaluable in media stereotyping scholarship. However, scant research examines media effects on subtle prejudice (Abraham & Appiah, 2006; Goidel, Parent, & Mann, 2011; Knobloch-Westerwick & Taylor, 2008).

Symbolic racism is measured with items targeting themes such as the denial that discrimination persists, the attitude that individual work ethic is tied to responsibility for outcomes, the perception that racial minorities (particularly African Americans) are making excessive demands, and that they gain undeserved advantage (McConahay & Hough, 1976; Sears & Henry, 2003). Through system-justifying beliefs relating to American individualism and achievement, individuals assume that a level playing field has been achieved and that all racial groups have equal opportunities to succeed in the United States. Research shows that symbolic racism influences Whites' racial attitudes such that African American individualism is distinctly racialized and not simply indicative of adherence to individualism (Sidanius, Levin, van Laar, & Sears, 2008; Tarman & Sears, 2005).

Jhally and Lewis (1992) proposed the enlightened racism model that suggests that positive media portrayals of African Americans are interpreted in ways that increase perceptions that racial/ethnic minorities have achieved the American Dream. These perceptions strengthen symbolic racist beliefs that discrimination is no longer a problem and that racial/ethnic out-groups are pushing too hard for their rights (Gaertner & Dovidio, 1986; McConahay, 1986; Sears, 1988). These studies suggest that viewers interpret and remember information in ways that fit with their existing beliefs and schemata.

Research on aversive racism explains that Americans often experience racial ambivalence; although they might openly endorse nonprejudiced egalitarian attitudes, they still harbor negative anti-Black feelings. Whereas blatant prejudice is characterized by antipathy and hate, aversive racism manifests subtly. Aversive racism begets evaluation biases in selection decisions, interpersonal judgments, and policy opinions (Dovidio & Gaertner, 2004; Pearson, Dovidio, & Gaertner, 2009). Studies show that aversive racists are negatively biased against Black candidates during hiring and promotion when the candidate's performance is ambiguous rather than impeccable. In other words, when a Black person is presented as flawless, aversive racists will likely not demonstrate any significant racial biases. However, if there is even a hint of ambiguity, aversive racists are likely to judge Blacks in harsher terms than Whites (Dovidio & Gaertner, 2004). In sum, negative framing of Black leaders such as Obama might encourage aversive racists to express their anti-Black sentiments without compunction.

Counter-stereotypic exemplars, implicit attitudes, and Black celebrities

Obama is often framed as a counter-stereotype in media, a public figure who can both lessen stereotype threat among African Americans and mitigate implicit racial bias among White Americans (Lane & Jost, 2011). Counter-stereotypical exemplars provide a unique contrasting opportunity to examine how steadfast media audiences rely upon racialized nuances to interpret and express liking of media celebrities. Researchers concerned with counter-stereotypical media figures predict that "consistent exposure to a Black male who is both counter-stereotypical in many ways and in a position of authority may serve to decrease Americans' automatic negative reactions to and evaluations of Black men more generally" (Richeson & Bean, 2011, p. 100).

The existing literature on the effects of counter-stereotypical exemplars on audience attitudes presents somewhat contradictory findings (Bodenhausen, Schwarz, Bess, & Wänke, 1995; Coover, 2001; Dasgupta & Greewald, 2001; Mastro et al., 2005; Ramasubramanian, 2015). Early pivotal research from the generalized appraisal perspective demonstrated that Black celebrities who are liked and respected (e.g., Oprah Winfrey, Colin Powell) elicited more favorable responses from White participants to Blacks both explicitly (Bodenhausen et al., 1995) and implicitly (Dasgupta & Greenwald, 2001). Another study found that participants who viewed stimuli of Black male lawyers associated Black Americans less readily with negative concepts and more readily with positive concepts than participants who viewed stimuli of Black male inmates (Barden, Maddux, Petty, & Brewer, 2004). The findings, however, are limiting because the effects lasted as long as participants were not conscious of the exemplars' atypicality. The logic that consistent exposure, such as through media, to counter-stereotypical images, such as President Obama, should reduce automatic racial bias among audiences has found inconsistent support (Richeson & Bean, 2011).

Fiske, Bergsieker, Russell, and Williams (2009) found evidence for three patterns that Whites rely on to interpret Black Americans through their study of Obama as a counter-stereotypical exemplar: stereotyping by omission (i.e., accentuating the positive but implying negativity by its absence), subtyping by class (i.e., social class and elite status as an educated, polished political figure which positions Obama as either an atypical Black American or an American "like us" who happens to be Black), and habituating (i.e., getting used to him) by exposure. Liking and respecting (see Fiske, Xu, Cuddy, & Glick, 1999) are fundamental social cognition dimensions that explain how these specific patterns function when non-Black audiences interpret Obama. Obama may be read as competent due to his credentials and somewhat warm due to his calm, passionate, and charismatic demeanor (Fiske et al., 2009). These findings suggest that rather than overcome and replace negative stereotypes with positive traits, individuals tend to simply leave out negative stereotypes.

Plant et al. (2009) explored how routine and high levels of exposure to Obama potentially influence non-Blacks' tendencies to prejudice and stereotype Blacks. They reason that participants recalled the positive Black exemplars (i.e., Obama) and perceived others would too when thinking of Black people, which resulted in drastically decreased levels of implicit anti-Black prejudice. Similarly, Columb and Plant (2011) found that activating positive qualities linked with Obama as a counter-stereotype led participants to exhibit significantly lower levels of implicit prejudice; extensive exposure to Obama resulted in a drop in implicit bias.

In contrast, Schmidt and Nosek (2010) examined a large heterogeneous sample of participants' attitudes before, during, and after the 2008 election season and observed very little systematic change for particular dates in the timeline, within subgroups of participants, and in implicit and explicit racial attitudes generally. The researchers posit that racial attitudes are malleable and conditional on complex features beyond the presence of a high profile, positive, counter-stereotypic exemplar such as Obama. Similarly, Fiske et al. (2009) concluded that, unless Whites routinely see a broad array of exemplary Black Americans, positive views of Black Americans may not extend to those they encounter in everyday life. Audiences may engage in a distancing process in interpretations of counter-stereotype exemplars like Obama from the collective racial group (i.e., Black Americans) and see them instead as exceptions, which creates a highly unlikely reality that audiences would lessen or dissociate the connection between other Black men and negative associations of threat and danger (Richeson & Bean, 2011). Importantly, these results should be tempered because "the salience of Obama has caused certain anti-egalitarian beliefs and ideologies to change in a negative manner, decreasing support for social policies that would benefit African Americans as a broader collective racial group" (Ashburn-Nardo, Livingston, & Waytz, 2011, p. 39).

Racialized scrutiny, tokenism, and presidential burdens

Research from organizational communication and leadership studies suggests that several situational and motivational factors influence how leaders from minority groups are framed and judged. Minority leaders are often perceived as "tokens" within their organizations. Tokens are a small number of individuals (typically less than 15%) from a minority group employed in positions traditionally occupied by majority group members (Kanter, 1977). Niemann (2003) defined racial tokenism as "a situation that handicaps members of racial/ethnic minority groups who find themselves working alone or nearly alone among members of another social category" (p. 100). Tokens are treated as representatives of the group that they belong to rather than as individuals, making them hyper-visible, heavily scrutinized, and likely to experience performance pressure (Kanter, 1977). Tokenism is gendered and racialized in ways that go beyond the logic of quantitative numbers (Wingfield & Wingfield, 2014). Research shows that Black leaders in token roles in majority White organizations experience tremendous stress because of a sense of isolation and the need to demonstrate greater levels of competence than their White peers (Jackson et al., 1995).

One of the stressors that such leaders experience is hyper-scrutiny from both internal and external audiences because of heightened visibility. Wingfield and Wingfield (2014) explained that actions, decisions, and even the appearance of those in token authority positions are monitored closely and constantly. Under such enhanced scrutiny, minor errors are magnified and likely to be made known more publicly than those of their counterparts from majority groups. Black leaders in their sample reported that they were held to a higher bar of expectations, had a smaller margin for errors, and had to bear more severe costs for missteps compared to White colleagues. We refer to this heightened visibility as *racialized scrutiny*.

Cook and Glass (2013) discussed bottom-up ascription, where the rationale for appointment of Black leaders to top-level positions is primarily to match the racial demographics of subordinates in the organization. Their research shows that such appointments are often made when an organization is not performing too well, a phenomenon that they label the *glass cliff effect*. Minority leaders typically experience resistance from both peers and subordinates, invariably losing popularity as a leader and ultimately framed as a failure. Their tenure is often followed by a search for a White male organizational savior who can bring stability to the failing organization.

Applying these ideas to the presidential office in the United States, Vaughn and Mercieca (2014) described three types of presidential burdens: "institutional burdens (the "glorious burdens" specific to the office of the presidency itself); contextual burdens (burdens specific to the historic moment when the president assumes office); and personal burdens (burdens specific to the man or woman who becomes president)" (p. 2). The expectations that American citizens have of their president are shaped by the ways in which public discourse, especially in the news media, portray presidential leaders. In the case of President Obama, the central aspect of his personal burden has focused on his race, which often intersects with institutional and contextual burdens. Race has been the primary lens used by the media to cover his presidency. Obama's largely post-racial approach to politics has resulted in critiques from both Conservatives and the African American community for not living up to their expectations.

Leadership studies, presidential rhetoric, and management sciences literature suggests that Black leaders such as Obama will be racially scrutinized and their behaviors will be seen as representative of the entire group to which they belong. However, few studies have examined the effects of portrayals of token leaders on the attitudes of majority group members towards minority groups. This study attempts to fill this gap by examining the effects of news media portrayals of President Obama as successful and popular (i.e., positive framing) versus unsuccessful and unpopular (i.e., negative framing) on Whites' evaluations of African Americans as a whole.

The present study

In sum, the theoretical perspectives relating to media framing of leaders from minority groups, priming effects of counter-stereotypical exemplars, racialized scrutiny of token leaders, and symbolic racism examined thus far suggest that exposure to media celebrities from racial/ethnic outgroups will likely influence Whites' racial attitudes. These effects are likely to differ by the ways in which these leaders are framed—as positive or negative. We expect that White participants are likely to express symbolic racism towards token Black leaders when these leaders are framed negatively, giving them reason to express their subtle aversive racism without appearing prejudiced. Although positive news stories that depict Obama in a positive light are unlikely to have a significant effect on audiences' racial attitudes, theoretically, we would expect negative news stories about Obama that depict him as unpopular and unsuccessful to activate underlying anti-Black affect and stereotypical perceptions of African Americans, which will indirectly lead to increased symbolic racist beliefs. In other words, we expect to find differential effects of positive versus negative Obama news stories to influence symbolic racist beliefs and predict that this relationship will be mediated by stereotypical beliefs and anti-Black affect. Therefore, our formal hypothesized model follows:

> Exposure to negatively framed Obama news stories as compared to positively framed stories will result in greater anti-Black affect and increased stereotypical perceptions of African Americans, which will lead to increased symbolic racist beliefs.

Method

To test the research hypothesis, the current study used a between-participants experimental design where participants were exposed to either positive or negative news stories about President Obama. After reading the news stories in the "News Enjoyment Study," respondents completed a "Quality of Life" questionnaire that included the dependent variables: stereotypical perceptions, prejudicial feelings, racial beliefs, and demographic information.

Participants

Participants in the current study included undergraduates ($N = 168$) enrolled in two mass lecture Communication courses at a large public university. They were between the ages of 18 and 30 ($M = 20.9$; $SE = 1.33$). Females compose the majority of the sample at 65.1%. In terms of racial/ethnic identification, 75.4% of participants are non-Hispanic Whites, 12% are Hispanic, 7.8% marked Other, 3% are Asian, 1.2% are African American, and 0.6% are Pacific Islanders. Because the hypotheses focused on White respondents' racial attitudes, data obtained from other racial minority group members were excluded from further analysis.

Procedure

After obtaining IRB approval, undergraduate students were recruited to participate in two unrelated studies: "News Enjoyment" and "Quality of Life." They received an email survey link to the studies. Participants were randomly assigned to either the positive or negative Obama story condition in the between-participants design. They were given a week's time to complete the studies in one single sitting of about 30 minutes at their convenience. Participants received extra credit for completing the survey. An alternative assignment was available for those who could not participate in the study.

In the first study, participants read three short news stories, each formatted in columns with a headline and one image, and then responded to items about the stories that assessed informative, enjoyable, interesting, and boring perceptions. In the second study, participants completed a Group Traits and Characteristics section that asked about their opinions about White Americans and African Americans, respectively. A list of various traits was presented on a grid-like format to which participants responded on a 7-point Likert-scale ranging from 1 (*strongly disagree*) to 7 (*strongly agree*). Similarly, the next set of questions prompted participants to convey their feelings towards members of the two racial groups on a 7-point Likert-scale ranging from 1 (*strongly disagree*) to 7 (*strongly agree*); this section included a variety of adjectives about emotions relating to out-groups such as fear, anger, and discomfort. The next subsection presented possible reasons accounting for political and economic progress for African Americans including symbolic racism questions relating to economic contributions, equal rights, and discrimination. Then, participants were asked about their general beliefs pertaining to the U.S. justice system followed by their likelihood to perform certain political actions. The preceding sections intended to measure quality of life indicators related to stereotypical beliefs and prejudicial feelings. Lastly, participants completed demographic information such as gender, age, race/ethnicity, and media usage.

Stimuli

The final experiment contained two sets of manipulated news stories. Participants were randomly assigned to one of two conditions: positive Obama story or negative Obama story. They were asked to read and respond to a positive or negative news story about Obama. The news judgment study also contained two neutral news stories chosen for inclusion in the final experiment: one story about the galaxy and another about pumpkin pie. The neutral stories were placed as fillers in each condition. Participants provided their thoughts on each news story's content and tone. Participants were asked, "Please indicate your responses to the story you just read." They were presented with a 7-point Likert-scale ranging from 1 (*strongly disagree*) to 7 (*strongly agree*) asking the extent to which they found each story informative, enjoyable, boring, and interesting. The main aim of this section was simply to prime participants to the Obama stories.

Both the news stories about Obama were manipulated to be identical in format to control for all visual elements such as headline positioning, type of photograph, photograph placement, font type, and size. Both the positive and negative news stories were one page in length, spread across two columns, with an image of the president shown with a smiling headshot with an American flag background. To increase the external validity of the stimuli, the news stories used were edited from existing published news articles; we did not invent our own positive or negative news story about Obama but edited pre-existing materials. We intentionally selected stories that were not the most popular so participants would not have likely read about them earlier nor did we select stories on highly controversial issues about which participants may have strong pre-existing attitudes.

Based on the existing literature on racialized scrutiny and tokenism, news stories that frame token minority leaders in authority positions as successful would likely be viewed positively. In contrast, news stories that portray such leaders as failing to meet expectations would likely be seen as negatively framed. Therefore, the positively framed news story about Obama in our study focused on his success and increasing popularity. It featured Obama being praised by the Brazilian president as a shrewd global leader whose policies are likely to significantly improve the relationship between the United States and Latin America. In contrast, the negatively framed news story was about his failure and decreasing popularity as a president. The focus of this news story was about how President Obama was resorting to appearing in television shows such as *Myth Busters* and *The View* to desperately curb his waning popularity.

Dependent variables

Anti-Black affect

The present study captures the affective aspects of racial attitudes by including prejudicial feelings as an outcome variable. Research on symbolic racism and aversive forms of subtle prejudice suggest that even those individuals who identify as non-prejudiced often harbor anti-Black feelings, which are likely to surface when the target of evaluation displays mixed competencies and when race is not the only factor that could account for harsher judgments. To assess such emotions, participants were asked, "Please look at each of the following adjectives to indicate how well they describe your feelings toward African Americans in general. Please be frank in your opinions." A 7-point Likert-type scale ranging from 1 (*strongly disagree*) to 7 (*strongly agree*) was used. The following types of items were included—dislike, disgust, anger, fear, nervous, and discomfort (Cronbach's $\alpha = 0.86$). These measures were based on previous work on intergroup emotions (Katz & Hass, 1988; Ramasubramanian, 2011).

Stereotypical perceptions

Participants were asked, "Indicate the extent to which you agree that the following traits describe African Americans/Black people in general. Please be honest in your responses." They responded to these items on a 7-point Likert-type scale ranging from 1 (*strongly disagree*) to 7 (*strongly agree*). The items included criminal, violent, drug dealer, drug user, lazy, poor, welfare recipient, and uneducated (Cronbach's $\alpha = 0.80$). These items were derived from prior research on cultural stereotypes of African Americans (Tan, Fujioka, & Tan, 2000; Mastro, 2000).

Symbolic racism

The items used to measure symbolic racism beliefs were derived from prior research (Sears & Henry, 2003; Tarman & Sears, 2005). The items thematically relate to the following subcategories on symbolic racism and stereotypes: excessive demands, denial of discrimination, and undeserved (dis)advantage. Participants were asked, "Please indicate the extent to which you agree with the following statements about African Americans. Please be honest in your responses." Participants responded on a 7-point Likert-type scale ranging from 1 (*strongly disagree*) to 7 (*strongly agree*).

The items for this measure follow (Cronbach's $\alpha = 0.70$): "African Americans are getting too demanding in their push for equal rights"; "Discrimination against African Americans is no longer a problem in the United States"; "African Americans generally do not complain as much as they should about their situation in society (reverse-coded)"; "African Americans contribute a great deal to the U.S. economy (reverse-coded)"; "Over the past few years African Americans have gotten more economically and politically than they deserve."

Results

Data analysis steps

The first step was to conduct correlational analyses to examine the relationships among the primary variables of interest. These analyses identified the degree to which the dependent variables correlated with one another. After this step, a multivariate analysis of variance was conducted to determine which dependent variables significantly correlated with the independent variable. The relative effects of various dependent variables on the independent variable were revealed in this step. Finally, to assess the simultaneous direct and indirect effects of the exogenous variable on the endogenous variables and to build a causal chain of links amongst these variables, a path analysis was conducted.

Preliminary analyses

An analysis of the descriptive statistics revealed the following means and standard deviations for the dependent variables, stereotypical perceptions ($M = 4.56$, $SD = 0.88$), anti-Black affect ($M = 3.09$, $SD = 1.33$), and symbolic racist beliefs ($M = 3.53$, $SD = 1.16$) on a 7-point Likert-type scale ranging from 1 (*strongly disagree*) to 7 (*strongly agree*). Overall, stereotypical perceptions were significantly higher compared to anti-Black affect and symbolic racist beliefs. Examining the Pearson's correlation coefficients for the bivariate correlational analysis revealed several significant moderate correlations in line with prior research. As expected, stereotypical perceptions and anti-Black affect were positively and significantly correlated ($r = 0.38$; $p < 0.01$); stereotypical perceptions and symbolic racist beliefs were positively correlated ($r = 0.40$; $p < 0.01$); and anti-Black affect and symbolic racism were positively correlated ($r = 0.24$; $p < 0.01$). Given the range of the correlations, we concluded that although these variables are reasonably correlated, they are also theoretically distinct from one another, making them appropriate for further analyses.

A multivariate analysis of variance was used to examine the effects of the independent variable (type of Obama story) on the dependent variables (anti-Black affect, stereotypical perceptions, and symbolic racist beliefs). It revealed a significant main effect for type of Obama story on anti-Black affect such that anti-Black affect scores for participants who read the negatively framed story ($M = 3.29$, $SD = 1.20$) were significantly higher than those who read the positively framed Obama story ($M =$

2.82, $SD = 1.43$); no other main effects or interaction effects were observed and the overall model was not statistically significant; Wilks' $\Lambda = 0.964$; $F(3, 120) = 1.473$; $p =$ n.s.; $\eta^2 = 0.036$.

Path analysis results

The final step, a path analysis, used AMOS to simultaneously examine the direct and indirect effects of the exogenous variable (type of Obama story: positive or negative) on the endogenous variables (stereotypical perceptions, anti-Black affect, and symbolic racist beliefs). The exogenous variables were dummy-coded such that 0 = positive and 1 = negative. The initial model used the observed variable approach to hypothesize direct and indirect correlations among all endogenous variables with the exogenous variable. The final model eliminated all paths that are not statistically significant at $p < 0.05$. These non-significant paths are indicated by dotted lines in the final model (see Figure 1). Goodness of fit of the final model was determined using a variety of indicators such as chi-square/df value over 0.05, the root mean square of approximation (RMSEA) less than 0.06, and a comparative fit index (CFI) higher than 0.95 (Hu & Bentler, 1999). The final developed path model fit well with the data as evidenced by $\chi^2 = 0.028$; $df = 1$; $p = 0.87$; CFI $= 1.00$; NFI $= 0.998$; RMSEA $= 0.000$ (0.000 to 0.114).

If we look at the individual paths in the final model generated in Figure 1, we notice a direct path from type of Obama story to anti-Black affect that shows a significant, positive correlation ($\beta = 0.48$; $p < 0.05$). When participants read negatively framed news stories about Obama as compared to positive ones, anti-Black affect was increased. In the next step of the final path diagram, we note a significant relationship between anti-Black affect and symbolic racist attitudes ($\beta = 0.21$; $p < 0.01$), suggesting that as anti-Black affect increases, symbolic racist beliefs also increase. Although the original hypothesized model included stereotypical perceptions of African Americans, this potential mediator was removed from the final

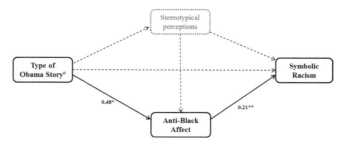

Figure 1. Final model illustrating the effects of type of news framing of Obama on anti-Black affect, stereotypical perceptions, and symbolic racist beliefs. $\chi^2 = .028$; $df = 1$; $p = .87$; comparative fit index $= 1.00$; normed fit index $= 0.998$; root mean square error of approximation $= .000$ (.000 to .114). Bold lines in the model indicate statistically significant relationships at $p < .05$ level; dotted lines indicate nonsignificant relationships between the variables. *$p < .05$; **$p < .01$. #Positive Obama Story $= 0$; Negative Obama Story $= 1$.

model (as indicated by the dotted line in Figure 1) as there was no significant relationship between the type of Obama story and the stereotypical perceptions. These findings reveal that the relationship between the type of news frames portraying Obama and the symbolic racist beliefs that they activate is mediated by anti-Black affect toward African Americans.

Discussion

We predicted that exposure to negatively framed Obama news stories compared to positively-framed news stories would result in increased stereotypical perceptions toward African Americans, more anti-Black affect, and greater symbolic racist beliefs. Our final model with significant findings reveals that when participants read negatively news stories about Obama, anti-Black affect and symbolic racist beliefs increased. The type of Obama story did not affect participants' stereotypical perceptions of African Americans but did influence their prejudicial feelings toward African Americans as a whole, which in turn increased symbolic racist beliefs. These findings have theoretical and practical implications for race/ethnic studies, journalism, political communication, and leadership studies.

President Obama undoubtedly serves as a unique case study for examining the influences of news framing of minority leaders due to his intersectional embodied identities as an accomplished politician in the highest office. As the first African American president of the United States, Obama has to bear the personal burden of being viewed through the lens of his cultural identity as a Black man. Our findings suggest that news stories featuring a counter-stereotypical exemplar can lead to differential effects on racial attitudes based on how s/he is framed in the media. The negatively-framed news stories about Obama resulted in an increase in anti-Black affect and symbolic racist beliefs. The negative media stereotypes and framing typically applied to members of a group—Black men, in the case of Obama—are more readily recalled and activated even when the focus of a particular news story concerns a strong counter-stereotypical exemplar from the outgroup, especially if the news story exudes negativity. The higher the visibility of the nontraditional leader, the more tokenized and perceived as exceptional compared to the larger racial group (i.e., Black Americans) the exemplar is seen.

The findings from this study contradict the idea that there is a sharp decline in Whites' prejudicial feelings about African Americans in this post-racial era where discrimination has faded away, giving rise to overall equality and inclusion. They challenge the common assumption in contemporary American society that racism is no longer a problem and that we live in a society where race no longer matters. Even subtle framing of news stories implicitly yet effectively invokes deeply embedded anti-Black affect. This finding supports the notion that symbolic racist beliefs relating to African Americans are so deeply entrenched in the social psyche of the U.S., that biases, prejudices and stereotypes against African Americans persist. Through indirect, implicit visual and verbal cues, the media continues to rehash and circulate racial/ethnic prejudices, which go unexamined and taken-for-granted as benign.

The mere exposure to negatively-framed news stories about Obama appears to be sufficient to activate racial/ethnic prejudices and symbolic racism. These vivid and concrete media exemplars invoke spontaneous negative feelings such as discomfort, dislike, and fear. Such implicit priming of anti-Black sentiments by media exemplars relies upon readers' existing associative networks of thoughts, emotions, and beliefs. Exposure to these media exemplars makes these mental models and schemas cognitively accessible and readily available for making generalized appraisals about the entire group. Through socialization processes over several generations, racial schemas are a significant part of the American psyche, making them very well-learned and highly accessible. Readers often subconsciously apply these primed feelings and thoughts in real-life contexts. More specifically, even those who consider themselves nonprejudiced routinely provide biased estimates of real-world occurrences of disproportionate media portrayals and evaluate ambiguous members of a target group in prejudiced ways.

Enlightened racism might undergird the process that leads White audiences to display symbolic racist attitudes upon negative news media exposure due to the consistency in seeing Obama, a counter-stereotype in many ways, featured in news stories. White audiences may interpret Black personalities constantly featured in mainstream news as evidence that equality has been achieved, which explains the symbolic racist attitudes upon viewing the negative news stories; the anti-Black affect correlation with symbolic racism dismantles the enlightened racist evaluations based on the negative news stories' content because it restores the focus on racialized scrutiny as the basis for negative affect attached to negative media tone.

The study findings support and extend existing literature from leadership studies that suggest that Black leaders in powerful positions of authority are often subject to tokenism, racialized scrutiny, and glass cliff effects. They help explain how, unless a high profile, powerful, authoritative leader from a minority group is nearly flawless, the individual is prone to harsher judgments based on closer racialized scrutiny, leaving little room for error before the seemingly positive counter-stereotype exemplar is reduced to negative, narrow attributes seen as more (stereo)typical of the broader collective group to which the leader belongs. Because of barriers such as discrimination, implicit biases, and lack of personal networks, it has been challenging for Blacks to be hired or promoted to top leadership positions in several organizations. Even if they do break the ceiling, as President Obama did, it is hard for token leaders to sustain popularity, especially during times of crises, when they are likely to be viewed more negatively and given lesser benefit of doubt than their White counterparts. Our findings contribute to this body of scholarship by conceptualizing racialized scrutiny as a useful concept for further exploration. They also provide empirical evidence for the hypothesis that framing of token leaders in authority positions leads to a generalized appraisal of the entire minority group to which they belong.

Aversive racism helps to explain the findings in terms of evaluation biases of African American targets when they are framed as unpopular and unsuccessful. Aversive racists might not consider themselves prejudiced and will otherwise be unbiased in judgments when Black targets are seen as having an impeccable record. However, whenever there is room for ambiguity and the social norm allows for negative evaluation of a candidate from a racial minority group, they more readily express anti-Black sentiment and racial biases. Although positive frames of token leaders might neither help nor hurt how they are judged, negative framing will likely lead to unfavorable evaluations of the entire minority group that they represent.

Automatic negative stereotype adherence occurs perhaps due to the subconscious atypicality of the exemplar (Barden et al., 2004) and the familiarity of negative stereotypes associated with the group, particularly when the news framing is negative. Negative stereotypes and feelings toward the minority group may be powerful enough to trump the counter-stereotypicality of the exemplars, thereby rendering them to a token status subject to heightened racialized scrutiny activated by negative news framing. Exposure (i.e., habituation) to more positive media frames of Black Americans in authority positions in addition to more real world contact with diverse Black Americans form the two-way, mutually reinforcing contexts likely to fuel an eventual overall decrease in prejudicial feelings. It appears that when prominent counter-stereotypical exemplars are relegated to exceptional token status and dominant out-group (i.e., White American) media audiences do not routinely see a broad spectrum of Black Americans beyond media-framed stereotypes, the potential positive effects that may apply in everyday inter-group dynamics are limited. Consistent exposure to positive framing of nontraditional leaders may be key in lessening automatic interpretations that rest upon racial biases (Columb & Plant, 2011; Richeson & Bean, 2011). Further research is needed to examine these nuanced effects of negative and positive framing of counter-stereotypical exemplars.

The type of news story about Obama was not significant in predicting stereotypical perceptions of African Americans as a whole. One explanation for the nonsignificant finding aligns with the colorblind or enlightened racism tendencies that occupy a clear social desirability in collective American society today, particularly among White Americans to maintain a positive social standing concerning race. When prompted to respond to items about the extent to which they apply stereotypes to entire collective racial out-groups (i.e., African Americans), White participants are unlikely to admit harboring or display responses that would reveal stereotypical perceptions of entire racial groups. Because of the perceived social and perhaps class status exception Obama occupies as a Black man, a further plausible explanation is that rather than overcome negative stereotype information and replace it with positive stereotyping, White participants omitted negative stereotypes (Fiske et al., 2009). This implication should be tempered because positive news stories did not result in decreased anti-Black affect or symbolic racist beliefs, which demonstrate that positive media coupled with counter-stereotypical representation do not necessarily lead to positive outcomes.

The current study is not without limitations. Obama as a counter-stereotype who is also a high profile political figure and, arguably, media celebrity, presumably invokes the political bipartisan nature of American politics; the extent to which political orientation of the audiences influences the evaluations of the first Black president is unclear. More research is needed in the area of subtle forms of contemporary racism with regards to news effects. Future studies could include implicit measures of racial attitudes such as the Implicit Association Test and the Affective Misattribution Procedure beyond self-reported measures of racial attitudes. In addition, further studies should include non-student samples to increase generalizability and external validity. Tracking the effects of positive versus negative frames over the long term at different points of the presidential tenure is likely to reveal useful insights about the malleability of racial attitudes.

Another methodological consideration for future research could be to include a control condition with neutral portrayals of Obama that were neither positive nor negative so that we could understand if the negative framing hurts Black leaders such as Obama or if instead positive framing helps to negate existing cultural stereotypes. Although we do not measure baseline scores of participants' anti-Black and symbolic racist beliefs, this is not to suggest that Whites do not harbor negative feelings towards African Americans when not primed by news stories. The actual anti-Black and symbolic racism scores were closer to neutral rather than skewed towards higher scores. However, we were interested in change in scores primed by positive versus negative news stories rather than the actual baseline scores. Furthermore, one of the stories was on international affairs and the other was on flagging popularity. Ideally, both stories would be on the same topic. For the sake of external validity, we used existing stories rather than create new ones.

In terms of practical implications, the findings from the current study suggest that proactive steps need to be adopted in newsrooms to ensure that more responsible journalism is practiced so that the detrimental effects of negative framing of minority leaders through racialized scrutiny are avoided. Equally important is media literacy education for audiences that makes them conscious media users who question taken-for-granted media stereotypes and hold the media accountable for accurate programming. Prejudice reduction efforts should go beyond correcting blatant prejudices to making aversive racists aware of their biased evaluative judgments based on negative framing of Black leaders. Organizations committed to inclusive workplaces should go beyond focusing on hiring and promoting Black leaders to authority positions to instead find ways to help them flourish and thrive in such positions. Communication practices within such organizational contexts should avoid unfair scapegoating, racial scrutiny, and hypervigilance of minority leaders and focus instead on providing mentoring programs and professional networks for such leaders to alleviate token pressures.

Overall, the study findings suggest that it is important to understand Barack Obama's presidency through the lens of racial scrutiny and tokenism by examining the differential effects of positive versus negative news frames on audiences' racial attitudes. Mere exposure to positive or negative news stories about President Obama in our experiment influenced Whites' racial attitudes towards African Americans as a whole. Chronically accessible anti-Black affect was activated by simply priming negatively framed news stories of a counter-stereotypical exemplar, which in turn increased symbolic racist beliefs. The current study adds to the existing scholarship on heuristic effects of media framing of public figures, particularly minority leaders in powerful positions, thus contributing to the literature on race/ethnic studies, political communication, presidential framing, leadership studies, and media stereotyping.

References

Abraham, L., & Appiah, O. (2006). Framing news stories: The role of visual imagery in priming racial stereotypes. *The Howard Journal of Communications, 17*, 183–203.

Aronson, J., Jannone, S., McGlone, M., & Johnson-Campbell, T. (2009). The Obama effect: An experimental test. *Journal of Experimental Social Psychology, 45*, 957–960.

Ashburn-Nardo, L., Livingston, R., & Waytz, J. (2011). Implicit bias: a better metric for racial progress. In G. Parks & M. Hughey (Eds.). *The Obamas and a (post) racial America?* (pp. 30–45). New York, NY: Oxford University Press.

Barden, J., Maddux, W. W., Petty, R. E., & Brewer, M. B. (2004). Contextual moderation of racial bias: the impact of social roles on controlled and automatically activated attitudes. *Journal of Personality and Social Psychology, 87*(1), 5.

Bodenhausen, G. V., Schwarz, N., Bless, H., & Wänke, M. (1995). Effects of atypical exemplars on racial beliefs: Enlightened racism or generalized appraisals. *Journal of Experimental Social Psychology, 31*(1), 48–63.

Bogle, D. (2001). *Toms, coons, mulattoes, mammies, and bucks: An interpretive history of Blacks in American films*. New York, NY: Continuum.

Brown Givens, S. M., & Monahan, J. L. (2005). Priming Mammies, jezebels, and other controlling images: An examination of the influence of mediated stereotypes on perceptions of an African American woman. *Media Psychology, 7*, 87–106.

Cashmore, E. (2012). *Beyond Black*. London, England: Bloomsbury Academic.

Columb, C., & Plant, E. A. (2011). Revisiting the Obama effect: Exposure to Obama reduces implicit prejudice. *Journal of Experimental Social Psychology, 47*, 499–501.

Cook, A., & Glass, C. (2013). Glass cliffs and organizational saviors: Barriers to minority leadership in work organizations? *Social Problems, 60*, 168–187.

Coover, G. (2001). Television and social identity: Race representation as "White" accommodation. *Journal of Broadcasting and Electronic Media, 45*, 413–441.

Dasgupta, N., & Greenwald, A. G. (2001). On the malleability of automatic attitudes: combating automatic prejudice with images of admired and disliked individuals. *Journal of Personality and Social Psychology, 81*, 800.

Dixon, T. L. (2005). Skin tone, crime news, and social reality judgments: Priming the stereotype of the dark and dangerous Black criminal. *Journal of Applied Social Psychology, 35*, 1555.

Dixon, T. L., & Linz, D. (2000). Overrepresentation and underrepresentation of African Americans and Latinos as lawbreakers on television news. *Journal of Communication, 50*, 131–154.

Dovidio, J. F., & Gaertner, S. L. (2004). Aversive racism. In M. P. Zanna (Ed.), *Advances in experimental social psychology* (Vol. 36, pp. 1–51). San Diego, CA: Academic Press.

Dovidio, J. F., Gaertner, S. L., Saguy, T., & Hehman, E. (2011). Obama's potential to transform the racial attitudes of White Americans. In G. S. Parks & M. W. Hughey (Eds.), *The Obamas and a (post) racial America?* (pp. 245–262). New York, NY: Oxford University Press.

Entman, R. M., & Rojecki, A. (2000). *The Black image in the White mind: Media and race in America*. Chicago, IL: University of Chicago Press.

Fiske, S. T., Bergsieker, H. B., Russell, A. M., & Williams, L. (2009). Images of Black Americans. *Du Bois Review, 6*(1), 83–101. doi:10.1017/S1742058x0909002X

Fiske, S. T., Xu, J., Cuddy, A. C., & Glick, P. (1999). (Dis)respecting versus (dis)liking: Status and interdependence predict ambivalent stereotypes of competence and warmth. *Journal of Social Issues, 55,* 473–489.

Ford, T. E. (1997). Effects of stereotypical television portrayals of African-Americans on person perception. *Social Psychology Quarterly, 60,* 266–275.

Gaertner, S. L., & Dovidio, J. F. (1986). The aversive form of racism. In J. F. Dovidio & S. L. Gaertner (Eds.), *Prejudice, discrimination, and racism* (pp. 61–89). Orlando, FL: Academic Press.

Goidel, K., Parent, W., & Mann, B. (2011). Race, racial resentment, attentiveness to the news media, and public opinion toward the Jena Six. *Social Science Quarterly, 92*(1), 20–34.

Hu, L., & Bentler, P. M. (1999). Cutoff criteria for fit indexes in covariance structure analysis: Conventional criteria versus. *Structural Equation Modeling, 6*(1), 1–55.

Jackson, P. B., Thoits, P. A., & Taylor, H. F. (1995). Composition of the workplace and psychological well-being: The effects of tokenism on America's Black elite. *Social Forces, 74,* 543–557.

Jhally, S., & Lewis, J. (1992). *Enlightened racism: The Cosby Show, audiences, and the myth of the American dream.* Boulder, CO: Westview Press.

Kanter, R. M. (1977). Some effects of proportions on group life: Skewed sex ratios and responses to token women. *American Journal of Sociology, 82,* 965–990.

Katz, I., & Hass, R. G. (1988). Racial ambivalence and American value conflict: Correlational and priming studies of dual cognitive structures. *Journal of Personality and Social Psychology, 55,* 893.

Knobloch-Westerwick, S., & Taylor, L.D. (2008). The blame game: Elements of causal attribution and its impact on siding with agents in the news. *Communication Research, 35,* 723–744.

Lane, K. A., & Jost, J. T. (2011). Black man in the White House: Ideology and implicit racial bias in the age of Obama. In G. S. Parks, M. W. Hughey, & C. Ogletree (Eds.), *The Obamas and a (post) racial America?* (pp. 48–69). Oxford, England: Oxford University Press.

Logan, E. L. (2011). *"At this defining moment": Barack Obama's presidential candidacy and the new politics of race.* New York, NY: New York University Press.

Mastro, D. E. (2000). The portrayal of racial minorities on prime time television. *Journal of Broadcasting & Electronic Media, 44*(4), 690.

Mastro, D. E., Tamborini, R., & Hullett, C. R. (2005). Linking media to prototype activation and subsequent celebrity attraction: An application of self-categorization theory. *Communication Research, 32,* 323–348.

McConahay, J. B. (1986). Modern racism, ambivalence, and the Modern Racism Scale. In J. F. Dovidio & S. L. Gaertner (Eds.), *Prejudice, discrimination, and racism* (pp. 91–125). San Diego, CA: Academic Press.

McConahay, J. B., & Hough, J. C. (1976). Symbolic racism. *Journal of Social Issues, 32*(2), 23–45.

Niemann, Y. F. (2003). The psychology of tokenism: Psychosocial realities of faculty of color. In G. Bernal, J. E. Trimble, A. K. Burlew, & F. T. Leong (Eds.), *Handbook of racial and ethnic minority psychology* (pp. 100–118). Los Angeles, CA: Sage Publishing.

Plant, E. A., Devine, P. G., Cox, W. T. L., Columb, C., Miller, S. L., Goplen, J., & Peruche, B. M. (2009). The Obama effect: Decreasing implicit prejudice and stereotyping. *Journal of Experimental Social Psychology, 45,* 961–964.

Ramasubramanian, S. (2011). The impact of stereotypical versus counterstereotypical media exemplars on racial attitudes, causal attributions, and support for affirmative action. *Communication Research, 38,* 497–516.

Ramasubramanian, S. (2015). Using celebrity news stories to effectively reduce racial/ethnic prejudice. *Journal of Social Issues, 71,* 123–138.

Richeson, J. A. & Bean, M. G. (2011). Does Black and male still = threat in the age of Obama? In G. S. Parks, M. W. Hughey, & C. Ogletree (Eds.), *The Obamas and a (post) racial America?* (pp. 94–112). Oxford, England: Oxford University Press.

Scheufele, D. A. (1999). Framing as a theory of media effects. *Journal of Communication, 49*, 103–122.

Schmidt, K., & Nosek, B. A. (2010). Implicit (and explicit) racial attitudes barely changed during Barack Obamas presidential campaign and early presidency. *Journal of Experimental Social Psychology, 46*, 308–314.

Sears, D. O. (1988). Symbolic racism. In P. Katz & D. Taylor (Eds.), *Eliminating racism: Profiles in controversy* (pp. 53–84). New York, NY: Plenum Press.

Sears, D. O., & Henry, P. J. (2003). The origins of symbolic racism. *Journal of Personality and Social Psychology, 85*, 259–275.

Sears, D. O., & Henry, P. J. (2005). Over thirty sources later: A contemporary look at symbolic racism. *Advances in Experimental Social Psychology, 37*, 150.

Sidanius, J., Levin, S., van Laar, C., & Sears, D. O. (2008). *The diversity challenge: Social identity and intergroup relations on the college campus*. New York, NY: Russell Sage Foundation.

Tarman, C., & Sears, D. O. (2005). The conceptualization and measurement of symbolic racism. *The Journal of Politics, 67*, 731–761.

Tesler, M., & Sears, D. O. (2010). *Obama's race: The 2008 election and the dream of a post-racial America*. Chicago, IL: University of Chicago Press.

Valentino, N. A. (1999). Crime news and the priming of racial attitudes during evaluations of the president. *Public Opinion Quarterly, 63*, 293–320.

Vaughn, J. S., & Mercieca, J. R. (2014). *The rhetoric of heroic expectations: Establishing the Obama presidency* (No. 24). College Station, TX: Texas A&M University Press.

Wingfield, A. H., & Wingfield, J. H. (2014). When visibility hurts and helps: How intersections of race and gender shape Black professional men's experiences with tokenization. *Cultural Diversity and Ethnic Minority Psychology, 20*(4), 483.

Technicolor Racism or Caricature Assassination? Satirizing White Anxiety About the Obama Presidency

Elka M. Stevens and Tyson D. King-Meadows

ABSTRACT
Using the theory of iconography, this article deconstructs the "Politics of Fear" caricature of Barack and Michelle Obama, featured on the cover of *The New Yorker* magazine, to investigate White imagination about the couple's socio-cultural identities. Published before the 2008 Democratic nominating convention, the caricature set the couple within the Oval Office and depicted Barack in an Arab-style tunic bumping fists with an armed Angela Davis-esque Michelle dressed in fatigues. We examine defenses of the image as satire against anti-Obama caricatures. We also examine original and secondary survey data to uncover the determinants of support for the caricature. We argue that the caricature gave a unifying visual form to disparate trepidations about the Americanness and religious identity of the Obamas. Our article concludes by situating the controversy over the cover alongside longstanding suspicions by Whites that Barack Obama has deceived Americans about his religious identity and loyalty to American ideals.

Published shortly before the 2008 Democratic National Convention, the July 21, 2008 front cover of *The New Yorker* magazine featured a caricature of Barack and Michelle Obama. Entitled "The Politics of Fear," the caricature, set in the Oval Office, depicted Illinois U.S. Senator Barack Obama in an Arab-style tunic, bumping fists with Michelle. She wore camouflage pants and toted an AK-47-esque rifle. An American flag burned in the background (Blitt, 2008). The caricature was defended as satire of White trepidations about the Obamas. Many did not believe Barack had the cultural capital, experience, or orientation necessary to be the leader of America and of the free world and that Michelle was patriotic enough to be the First Lady and the primary confidant of the executive (Beinart, 2008; Joseph, 2011; Parlett, 2014).

The July 21st issue of *The New Yorker* instantly generated controversy and could not be dismissed as irrelevant (Banaji, 2008; Ressing, 2011). Owned by Condé Nast Publications, *The New Yorker* was a nontraditional news magazine whose currency amongst influential Americans was only rivaled by *The Economist* and *The Atlantic*

(*The New Yorker*, 2009). Its readership valued satire, caricatures, and commentary and shaped the electoral landscape (Pew Research Center, 2009). The issue was an immediate commercial success. Initially available through subscription and single-issue sales, the issue became available through e-commerce sites priced above the original single-issue cost of $4.50. As the *New York Post* noted, " …preliminary estimates [showed] single-copy sales surged 80 percent over average weekly newsstand sales, or around 75,000 copies, compared with average newsstand sales of around 43,000" (Kelly, 2008, para. 3). Condé Nast has kept the caricature in the public eye as a subject of debate and historical import, offering at least 11 different presentation styles of the cover at varying price points (Condé Nast Collection, 2016). The persistence of White trepidations about the "Americanness" of the Obamas places "The Politics of Fear" caricature as both a byproduct of the 2008 environment and a scholarly fulcrum from which to examine visual communication in racial/post-racial American politics (Joseph, 2011).

Using a different analytical approach than previous examinations of the cover, we integrate iconographical and survey data analyses to deconstruct the caricature and to explore public attitudes about the image. First, we situate the caricature within trepidations about the Obamas' identities and about Barack's intentions. Next, we outline how these anxieties provided fodder for the caricature and undergirded the magazine's defense. Third, we outline why iconography as visual content analysis enables the best syntax deconstruction of the caricature. Fourth, we conduct primary and secondary data analysis on surveys to explore opinion about the caricature and its meanings. Finally, we conclude by underscoring how the caricature may have solidified the Obamas' inability to dispel White belief in the "Barack is a Muslim" and "the Obamas are un-American" narratives. We connect these beliefs to White perceptions of the Obama Presidency and to the 2016 presidential election cycle.

Trepidations about the Obamas

Media outlets during the 2008 election cycle focused heavily on the Obamas' biographies and associational linkages. First, much was made of the racial, religious, and cultural identity of Senator Obama, and the extent to which he and Michelle expressed American patriotism. Barack's parental lineage, childhood in Indonesia and Hawaii, Muslim middle name, and his achievements were used as proxies for his "un-Americanness" and leadership potential. Barack's supporters pushed his aesthetic, "cultural hybridity," and his global-centric worldview, as the underpinning for the "biography as destiny" idea (Traub, 2007, para. 8). Opponents, including Democratic New York U.S. Senator Hillary Clinton and Republican Arizona U.S. Senator John McCain, countered that Barack's bicultural parentage and worldview would be liabilities if he had to draw upon an in-depth experiential-based understanding of American interests (Simien, 2016). Michelle's biography was also called into question. Detractors interpreted Michelle's biography and judgment as indicators of negative affect toward America. Michelle's Southside Chicago upbringing,

Princeton University senior thesis examining attitudes amongst the school's Black alumni, and membership in Rev. Jeremiah Wright's Trinity United Church of Christ were points of contention (Clayton, 2010). For some, Michelle epitomized "Black rage" about social stratification and racism, and Black ambivalence about America (Powell & Kantor, 2008). Opponents labeled Michelle in many ways, including as an "angry Black woman" and bitter (Harris-Perry, 2011; Mitchell, 2008; Powell & Kantor, 2008). Second, opponents called into question the Obamas' affiliations with Wright and William "Bill" Ayers, a former member of the Weather Underground. For detractors of the Obamas, their biographies suggested an emotional unwillingness or a cultural inability to embrace American ideals.

Such skepticism about the Obamas' manifested in public opinion before the 2008 convention. A March 2008 Pew Research Center survey showed that 10% of voters believed Barack to be Muslim. By September, that figure had risen to 13%; 17% of Whites without a college degree reporting having such a belief and 16% of White Evangelical Protestants believed Barack to be a Muslim (Pew Research Center, 2008a). Another survey found that 75% of Democratic and Democratic-leaning voters viewed Barack as patriotic. But there was a 10-point deficit relative to the percentage expressing a similar belief about Clinton (Pew Research Center, 2008b). Angst also revolved around Obama's hybridity. The fear of alien allegiance supplemented but did not supplant racial antipathy: Beinart (2008) noted, "Our national vernacular is filled with anti-Black euphemisms, but cosmopolitan isn't one of them. Yet when critics attack Barack, that's the word that keeps popping up." He continued, "Ever since the primaries, Obama's detractors have tried to depict him less as threatening to White America than as distant from America itself" (para. 5–6).

In all, two competing narratives emerged about the Obamas during the 2008 election cycle. Barack was either nonnative/un-American, or he was uniquely American. Michelle was either a Black anti-American radical, or she was an exceptional American. Supporters exalted the Obamas as prototypical Americans. Opponents exalted the Obamas as exemplars of anti-/un-Americanness.

The New Yorker cover as visual communication

A magazine's front cover is its most prominent and communicative message to its readership and advertisers. Publishers use the cover's layout of imagery and text to communicate and promote the editorial vision, create interest, and to increase sales (Johnson & Prijatel, 2000). An editorial decision to place an illustration, specifically caricatures and political cartoons, on the cover is not without consequence. A political cartoon features recognizable visual symbols and metaphors, visual distortion, irony, and, often, stereotypes (Bates, Lawrence & Cervenka, 2008; Conners, 2005; El Refaie, 2009). Similarly, a caricature is a stylized drawing that uses exaggeration or "ludicrous distortion" to enhance readily identifiable features and is inherently controversial ("Caricature," 2010). Its subject matter, context surrounding its dissemination and reception, and illustrator intention determine whether it can be considered a political cartoon. In short, its meaning is in the eye of the beholder, and placement on the front cover of a news magazine is not easily ignored.

Such was the case for *The New Yorker* cover. As a visual product, it reflected the normalized and exceptional nature of Barack's historic run. First, the Obamas were not beyond satirical approach. Second, unlike other presidential contenders of minority heritage, Barack was mathematically positioned to secure the nomination of a major political party. Competing narratives about race, patriotism, and allegiance therefore provided fodder for the caricature (Joseph, 2011; Rossing, 2011). Illustrator Barry Blitt entitled the caricature "The Politics of Fear" and the magazine claimed it intended to "satirize the use of scare tactics and misinformation in the Presidential election to derail Obama's campaign" (*The New Yorker*, 2008, para. 1). Editor David Remick defended the cover on NPR's *All Things Considered*. Remick claimed the cover was designed "to hold a pretty harsh light up to the rumors, innuendos, lies about the Obamas," such as, they are "insufficiently patriotic or soft on terrorism or any of the other things we've had to encounter." He continued, the cover is "a different vocabulary satire than essays or radio essay, but there it is" (Norris, 2008, para. 3). When asked about "mistruths" and "untruths" about presidential candidates, Remick remarked, "Well, when I look at poll numbers and I see that still sizable portions of the country believe this nonsense about Barack Obama, to me that's a very, very legitimate source of critique, of satire on our cover and anywhere else in the magazine" (Norris, 2008, para. 15). Blitt also defended the caricature in an interview with *Huffington Post,* writing, "I think the idea that the Obamas are branded as unpatriotic [let alone as terrorists] in certain sectors is preposterous. It seemed to me that depicting the concept would show it as the fear-mongering ridiculousness that it is" (Pitney, 2008, para. 1).

Many debunked *The New Yorker*'s defenses (Joseph, 2011; Rossing, 2011). Wingfield and Feagin (2009) exclaimed that the caricature was situated within a preexisting "white racial frame" that "portrays whites as inherently more moral, intelligent, kind, and hardworking than most people of color" (p. 13). The authors also noted, "the inside *New Yorker* article on Senator Obama made no effort to explain the satirical cover." This, they contended, made it likely that readers unfamiliar with the magazine would view the images "literally rather than satirically" (Wingfield & Feagin, 2009, p. 91). "Despite the *New Yorker* magazine's claim that the cover art was intended to be satirical and should be viewed as such," they continued, "ultimately the images of the Obamas as terrorists played into existing white-framed ideas of the Obamas as different and potentially dangerous threats to U.S. national security" (Wingfield & Feagin, 2009, p. 91).

The Obama campaign foreshadowed this analysis. In a July 2008 CNN interview, an Obama spokesperson said, "*The New Yorker* may think, as one of their staff explained to us, that their cover is a satirical lampoon of the caricature Sen. Obama's right-wing critics have tried to create … But most readers will see it as tasteless and offensive. And we agree" (Mooney, 2008, para. 3). In the same interview, an Obama supporter stated, "I think it's outrageous that we'd have a cover that would depict racism, sexism, anti-religion, also anti-patriotism, and then on top of it to try to draw a conclusion that Mr. Obama has some sympathy toward terrorism" (para. 9). Senator Obama put it more forcefully on *Larry King Live* on July 15, 2008. He noted the satire may have "fueled some misconceptions," and that Blitt was not "entirely successful" with his attempt to satire (Waters, 2008).

In short, competing narratives emerged about the cover (Rossing, 2011). For *The New Yorker*, the caricature was satire of anti-Obama caricatures. It had confidence in the public's willingness, ability, and desire to recognize the satire. For others, the caricature was character assassination because it packaged anti-Obama rhetoric into one colorful visual without providing viewers with an analytical framework to decipher the satire. To differentiate, we label the magazine's position as *caricature assassination,* and we label the counter position as *technicolor racism*. Although *technicolor* is associated with color cinematography, we use the term in its dual sense as a creative process and as an adjective. In that regard, detractors of the caricature saw it as a vivid amalgamation of varied takes on the Obamas' supposed cultural and psychic distance from White Americans, a modern-day expression of anti-Black racism different from outmoded expressions emphasizing biology and intellect. Given the reliance of these positions on visual and attitudinal analysis, we turn to iconography and survey data to explore public understanding of the caricature.

The lens of iconography

Visual content analysis is used to understand audio, visual, and verbal materials as "texts" that include images and related messages in magazines, political advertisements, and other media (van Leeuwen & Jewitt, 2005, p. 14). Van Leeuwen (2005) suggested iconography as a framework to extend content analysis to understand not only what these texts represent, but also to "understand the context in which the image is produced and circulated" (p. 92). Furthermore, iconography is concerned with "how and why cultural meanings and their visual expression come about historically" (van Leeuwen, 2005, p. 92). In all, iconography moves beyond semiotics by offering a deep contextualization of the image and its placement (i.e., historical location, receivership). Van Leeuwen (2005) and Müller and Özcan (2007) drew upon the iconographical work of Panofsky (1972) to further understanding and appreciation of art objects, including caricatures and political cartoons.

Erwin Panofsky's iconographical framework (hereafter iconography) provides a guideline for deconstructing a caricature as visual text. Iconography seeks to uncover what images represent, how these images are represented, and underlying ideals and values of images. Panofsky offers three layers of analysis to ascertain pictorial meaning: (a) representational meaning—what is shown, (b) iconographical symbolism—what it means, and (c) iconological symbolism—in what context it is situated (van Leeuwen, 2005).

Representational meaning is the identification of the featured subject(s) through visual intertextuality (van Leeuwen, 2005). This requires reference to the work's observable dimensions based upon viewers' experiences. In that, representational meaning is closely related to Barthes' concept of denotation in semiotics—the study of the symbol systems and acknowledgement of the content with respect to whom or what is shown (van Leeuwen, 2005).

Iconographical symbolism connects the subject matter to "themes or concepts" (Panofsky, 1972, p. 54). Identifying specific themes or concepts requires the "correct identification of motifs" or recurring elements as "prerequisite" steps (Panofsky, 1972, p. 8). According to van Leeuwen (2005), to identify a motif one must be concerned with how the text and context work in tandem to symbolize "people, places, and things" (p. 107). One must take particular note of the subject, expressive gestures, unexpected visuals and locales, and fantastic situations that suggest texts connected to a theme. Specifically, iconographical symbolism is an appropriate tool when motifs (a) are presented without obvious historic connection, (b) are frequently used or referenced, or (c) are used intentionally and symbolically (van Leeuwen, 2005).

Iconological symbolism aims to "ascertain those underlying principles which reveal the basic attitude of a nation, a period, a class, a religion, or a philosophical persuasion" (Panofsky, 1972, p. 55). Iconology asks researchers to contextualize the creation of the work and its reception (van Leeuwen, 2005). The perception of receivers and the intentions of the illustrator are important here. Context matters and includes receivership, production, and an interpretative lens. Consequently, this third layer focuses on the implicit and explicit attitudes connected to a visual text.

In conclusion, Panofsky's iconographical framework demands an understanding of the zeitgeist surrounding the text and demands attention to tensions within symbolic values or the inherent tensions between receiver and artist. The artist may intend to satirize, but may have cemented an underlying value structure within certain groups. Art, as a synthesis of form and context, involves intentional and unintentional intrinsic meaning (Bates, Lawrence, & Cervenka, 2008).

Methods

Our multimethod approach uses iconographic analysis to explore *The New Yorker* caricature as a communicative device and uses survey data analysis to ascertain public evaluation of this communication.

Iconographical analysis

We examine the formal composition of the cover and use content analysis to excavate the "relevant variables of representation" (Bell, 2005, p. 15). We then look to the motifs as reflecting concerns about the Obamas. Following that, we use iconological symbolism to examine thematic foci related to the Obamas' relational and ascriptive identities.

Survey analysis

We examine data from two national surveys to evaluate response to *The New Yorker* cover. The first is the News Interest Index from July 18 to July 21, 2008, a national telephone survey of 1,000 U.S. adults by the Pew Research Center for the People and the Press. The News Interest Index survey (hereafter Pew Data) measured news attentiveness, assessment of news stories, and attitudes about the caricature. However, the survey did not query attitudes and respondents who did not see the cover were excluded. Given these two limitations, we turn to the 2008 Congressional Cooperative Election Study (CCES) as the second survey. The 2008 CCES was an online survey of U.S. adults sampled from an opt-in panel managed by YouGov/Polimetrix. The survey queried social, racial, and political attitudes; vote choice; and candidate evaluation. It was fielded in October (pre-election) and November (post-election) and yielded a large sample size. YouGov weights its data to produce a national sample and state-level samples which are demographically representative. The American Association of Public Opinion Research cooperation and response rates were 78% and 47%, respectively (Ansolabehere, 2009). Using the thematic analysis from the iconographical framework, we developed and embedded a post-election task on a team module of the 2008 CCES survey (hereafter CCES data). All respondents were shown the full-color *New Yorker* cover. We used data from the 1,516 adults (1,150 non-Hispanic Whites, 157 Blacks, 140 Hispanics, and 71 other racial minorities) who participated in our module (King-Meadows, 2008). We examine both surveys using descriptive and multivariate regression analyses.

Evaluation of the caricature

The 2008 Pew Data contained several caricature-related questions. Respondents were first primed to think about news related to the presidential election and then asked how much they had "heard" about and if they had seen the cover. Sixty-seven percent heard "a lot or a little" about the cover, and 77% reported to have "seen the cover or a picture of it." Only the latter respondents ($N = 536$) were asked follow-up questions. The first was, "Do you think it was okay or not okay for the *New Yorker* to publish this magazine cover?" Subsequent questions asked if the following words "described the *New Yorker* cover or not": (a) offensive; (b) racist; (c) clever; and (d) funny. We coded responses so 1 represented agreement and 0 represented disagreement. All "don't know" responses were excluded. By contrast, our 2008 CCES survey task provided each respondent with the caricature and asked, "Which one of these statements do you think best describes this cover from *The New Yorker* magazine?" Respondents could select one of five statements: (a) "Barack Obama is a Muslim," (b) "Michelle Obama is a radical," (c) "The Obamas are violent," (d) "The Obamas are un-American," and (e) "The image conveys none of these statements." Respondents who skipped the question were excluded. Because respondents were given five competing descriptors, we interpret choice as an imperfect measure of the most salient theme. We coded choice as 1 and 0 otherwise.[1]

News attentivenes

We use two items in the Pew Data to measure news attentiveness. First, whether respondents came to a "more favorable opinion, a less favorable opinion," or had "no change in opinion" about Barack Obama and John McCain in the past few days.

We differentiated respondents by change in opinion about Obama: 0 (*Obama: No change*). Second, whether respondents "happened to follow each [of six] news [stories] very closely, fairly closely, not too closely, or not at all closely" the week prior to the survey, and which story they had "most closely" followed or if they had followed another story. They were (a) "Reports about the condition of the U.S. economy," (b) "Financial troubles for home mortgage lenders Fannie Mae and Freddie Mac," (c) "The current situation and events in Iraq," (d) "News about the candidates for the 2008 presidential election," (e) "The debate in Washington over U.S. energy policy," and (f) "The military effort in Afghanistan against Taliban fighters." We differentiated respondents who "most closely followed" news about Iraq or Afghanistan: 0 (*other news*), 1 (*followed Iraq*), 1 (*followed Afghanistan*). We use similar measures from the CCES Data. *News Interest* is measured by how much respondents followed "what's going on in government and public affairs." Responses ranged from 1 (*most of the time*) to 4 (*hardly at all*). To parallel the Iraq measure in the Pew Data, we use "Which comes closest to your opinion on U.S. decisions regarding Iraq?" Responses were 1 (*mistake from beginning*), 2 (*mistake worth the cost*), 3 (*right thing, mistakes made too costly*), 4 (*right thing, worth despite mistakes*), and 5 (*right thing, no mistakes*). We recoded so higher numbers represented stronger disagreement (*Iraq mistake*).

Racial and political attitudes

The CCES data contained measures not found in the Pew Data. We measured ideology from 1 (*very liberal*) to 5 (*very conservative*), but dummy coded the answers to differentiate respondents at the far ends of the spectrum (*Liberal* and *Conservative*). To account for religious identification and behavior, we created a religiosity index from four items: religious identification (0 = unaffiliated, 1 = otherwise), importance of religion (0 to 3), frequency of church attendance (0 to 5), and frequency of prayer (0 to 6). *Religiosity* ranged from 0 to 15 ($M = 8.70$, $SD = 4.53$). A thermometer score (*Warmth Toward Blacks*) proxies for anti-Black affect ($M = 75.17$, $SD = 21.69$). We coded self-reported 2008 presidential vote choice with 1 (*Obama voter*), 0 (*otherwise*). Non-voters were excluded.

Demographics

Dummy variables distinguished respondents by party: 1 (*Democrat*), 1 (*Republican*) and 0 (*other/Independent*). We also differentiated respondents by gender 1 (*female*) and by race. From the Pew Data, we measured education from 1 (*8th grade or less*) to 7 (*postgraduate degree*), age from 1 (*18–20*) to 13 (*75 and older*), and income from 1 (*less than $30k*) to 4 (*$75k or more*). From the CCES Data, we measured education from 1 (*did not graduate from high school*) to 6 (*postgraduate degree*), age from 1 (*18–34*) to 3 (*55 and older*), and income from 1 (*less than $10k*) to 14 (*$150k or more*). We controlled for residential location by distinguishing Pew respondents in the center city of metropolitan areas (Central City) and by distinguishing CCES respondents from the former confederacy (South).

Table 1. Iconographical Analysis of the Obamas in Blitt's "Politics of Fear" Caricature.

	Iconographical layers of pictorial meaning		
Motifs	Representational symbolism	Iconographical symbolism	Iconological symbolism
Barack Obama			
Husband of Michelle	Biracial man	U.S. President	Power
Tunic, pants, turban, sandals	Muslim dress	Closet Muslim	Foreign
Gaze toward viewer	Hidden knowledge	Inside joke	Deception
Hand gesture	Unique Communication	Agreement/conspiracy	Non-White culture
Michelle Obama			
Wife of Barack	Black Woman	U.S. First Lady	Influence
Camouflage & combat boots	Military attire	Covert operations	Conflict
Rifle & ammunition	AK-47 w/ strap	Soldier	Violence
Afro hairstyle	Angela Davis	Black Power Movement	Militant/Radical
Sly gaze	Hidden knowledge	Inside joke	Deception
American flag			
In Oval Office	Nation State	Patriotism	Power
Burning in fireplace	Desecration/disposal	Political speech	Anti-American
Under framed image	Adornment	Personalized space	Reverence
Near image of Muslim man	Patriarch	Osama Bin Laden	Enemy of America

Source. Authors' analysis employing Panofsky's (1972) Iconographical Analysis.

Results

We first detail results from our iconographical analysis. We next outline results from our survey data analysis. Results in Table 1 show that the caricature depicted the Obamas as culturally, emotionally, and attitudinally distant. Our results also show that attitudes were consistent with the anti-Obama themes uncovered in the visual analysis.

Social distance, modality, and behavior

First, *The New Yorker* cover would be characterized as having "far social distance" (Bell, 2005, p. 29). The full bodies of the Obamas are shown. Illustrations featuring a full body convey that the person is more exposed, suggesting less connection to the viewer. By contrast, at an intimate distance, one only sees the face or the head (Bell, 2005). Relatedly, *social distance* can also refer to the "amount of warmth, intimacy, indifference, or hostility" among groups (Marshall, 1998, para. 1). Hence, the Obamas share a moderate level of warmth and intimacy, as they are partially facing one another bumping fists, an interactive gesture. Second, the cover has "medium visual sensory modality" (Bell, 2005, p. 30). Although the image is in color, it uses pastels or less saturated colors, as opposed to using intense colors ("high") or Black and White ("low"). Third, the cover centralizes the couple's appearance and behavior—specifically their dress, gestures, poses, and gazes—making them the focal points (Hillestad, 1980). The image activates notions that wearing religious, national, or cultural dress is indicative of citizenship, affinities, or attitudes (Roach-Higgins & Eicher, 1992). The use of color, tonal shades, perceptual detail, and depth are also meant to draw and mute attention. In this regard, the caricature depicted the Obamas as connected to one another and disconnected from America/Americans.

Dress

The caricature depicted Barack wearing a turban on his head that appears to be similar to the turban of the person in the portrait above the fireplace. It covers most of his closely cropped hair. He is wearing a salwar kameez-style of outfit—consisting of an unbelted, plain, collarless, long sleeved, below-the-knee tunic, dark pants that taper just above the ankle and thinly-soled sandals. The choice of outfit is a deliberate attempt to communicate to the viewer that Barack is a Muslim, Islamist, or even a partner in a Mujahideen dyad (Tristam, 2008). Furthermore, this outfit draws upon debates about Barack's religiosity and legitimacy to be President. The cover channels the 2008 release of a photograph taken of Obama during a 2006 trip to Kenya and five other African countries (Associated Press, 2006). The photograph featured Barack in attire initially reported to be Muslim dress from Wajir, a rural city in northwest Kenya. A Somali newspaper reported that the cultural dress in the photograph was traditional garb "worn by bishops, rabbis in Ethiopia and (pagan) shepherds in the Horn of Africa" (National Public Radio, 2008). Although it is customary for visiting political leaders to adorn the garb of the nation being visited, such a gesture is expected for heads of state or ambassadors (Powell, 2008). Obama was neither. Detractors considered Barack's decision as a symbol of his non-Christian identity and a cavalier approach to America's security concerns. For some, Senator Clinton's release of the photo was anti-Obama fear-mongering (Joseph, 2008).

Second, Michelle was depicted as a clown-like, violent, relic of bygone eras. Blitt dressed Michelle in a long-sleeved blouse, camouflage-patterned pants, and large clown-like, military-style boots reminiscent of 1960s Black Power or the 1970s boots prevalent in nonheterosexual circles. She also wore an afro and shouldered a military rifle. These elements mimicked Black feminist, Black Panther Party member, and former FBI fugitive Angela Davis. Hence, Michelle, as depicted, is a Davis-esque solider willing to fight for a Black, radical, feminist, or anti-order agenda. The image was in deep contrast to the narratives proffered by Michelle's supporters: fashion icon, the next Jackie Kennedy, gentle, and personable. The caricature linked Michelle to symbols of death and revolution (Joseph 2011, Rossing, 2011).

The body

The New Yorker caricature played into gendered and racial stereotypes (Joseph, 2011; Rossing, 2011). With her head tilted and gazing upward toward Barack, Michelle's body is contorted—directed toward her husband and the viewer. This look could be classified as "demand/seduction," where she looks up, head canted and with cinched exaggerated lips toward the viewer (Bell, 2005, p. 31). Her right hand is balled in a fist and is extended to touch her husband's fist. Her other hand is on her hip with the palm facing outward and elbow forward, keeping the rifle behind her. An anonymous commenter on the internet referred to Michelle's gestures as a "Hezbollah-style fist jab, mouth twisted, [straight] out of Islam" (Beam, 2008, para. 3). Barack is positioned with his back partially to the viewer. His left arm and curled fist are extended. From the corner of his eye, he is looking over his left shoulder away from his wife, gazing toward the viewer. His full, closed lips and an oversized nose are prominent. His feet are shoulder-length apart. These distortions helped communicate distance from the (White) viewer.

In addition, the minimal text helped to frame the visual. The top of Michelle's afro and the top of Barack's turban obscured parts of the mast. Superimposed on the image were "Price $4.50" and "July 21, 2008." Other than the illustrator's signature and the universal product barcode, the cover featured no headline, subtext or additional information. Some copies featured a flap that covered the left half of the illustration, printed with the headline "How Obama Became a Pol" by Ryan Lizza.

Background

Five elements of the cover's background created a sense of depth about the physical setting and the characters in the foreground. First, the curved wall showed dimensionality. The shape of the carpet, curved walls, and furnishings reflected images of the present-day Oval Office. The Oval Office contextualized the Obamas in the foreground as residents and controllers of the space. Second, Blitt played to trepidations about non-White power by placing a burning American flag in the fireplace. The depiction worked on multiple levels. According to United States Code (4 U.S. Code 1, Section 8), the flag should never touch the ground, represents a living country, is a "living" thing, should never be used or displayed in a manner that it can be torn or soiled, and, if necessary, "should be destroyed in a dignified way, preferably by burning" (4 U.S. Code 1, Section 8). That the American president, as commander in chief, may modify or repeal rules pertaining to the flag makes the image evermore powerful, as does the acknowledgment that Supreme Court decisions define burning the flag as protected symbolic speech under the First Amendment (*Texas v. Johnson*, 1989; *United States v. Eichman*, 1990). The caricature intimated that a President Obama would desecrate the flag or burn it. Third, Blitt placed the burning flag under a fireplace portrait presumably of Osama Bin Laden. By positioning Bin Laden's image in a place of reverence, the caricature suggested Barack's affection for a man devoted to destroying America. Fourth, Blitt centered the "fist-bump" in the caricature—a gesture the couple made along the campaign trail. The Obamas "fist-bump of hope" as it is now known ("fist bump") took place on June 5, 2008, when, after a kiss on the cheek, a hug, and a few words, Michelle "raised her right fist, and Barack bumped it with his left" fist at a rally in Minnesota (McShane, 2008, para. 12). The fist-bump is akin to a visual colloquialism, situated within a long processional of hand-based gestures, that signifies affinity, agreement, congratulations, or partnership (Stephey, 2008). While this gesture is not confined to racial communities, it is racialized and associated with non-White culture. A Fox News anchor, E.D. Hill of "America's Pulse" show, likened the gesture to a "terrorist fist jab" and was soon relieved of duty afterwards (Beam, 2008; Rossing, 2011; Wallace, 2008). Fifth, the individual behavioral gazes suggested deception. Michelle's gaze is similar to the loving gaze she gave Barack when they completed the original fist bump. Barack's gaze conveys something sinister. Far from being surprised, Barack's gaze alludes to a cool, dismissive demeanor, as if gloating about the hidden information.

Table 2. Evaluation of *New Yorker* Cover by Race and Party Identification (Pew Data).

Group	Okay to publish	Offensive	Racist	Clever	Funny
Overall	.52	.55	.38	.37	.27
Race/ethnicity					
White	.56***	.52*	.35**	.38	.27
Black	.27	.71	.61	.30	.19
Other minority	.51	.63	.43	.38	.32
Latino	.51	.59	.36	.34	.32
Party Identification					
Democrat	.32***	.70***	.54***	.22***	.17***
Independent	.63	.48	.34**	.48	.35
Republican	.68***	.42***	.19***	.41***	.31***

Notes. DV = dependent variable. STATA 14 used for equations. Respondents are those who reported to have seen the cover. Source: News Interest Index, July 18–21, 2008, Pew Research Center (weighted data).
*$p < .05$. **$p < .01$. ***$p < .001$.

Taken together, our application of Panofsky's three layers of pictorial meaning underscores how effectively "The Politics of Fear" depicted public trepidations about the Obamas (as a unit) and about Michelle and Barack (as individuals). The caricature however gambled on whether individuals outside *The New Yorker*'s readership could decipher its attempt to satire anti-Obama anxiety (Joseph, 2001). We now turn to survey data to see if the public saw the cover as caricature assassination or technicolor racism.

Public attitudes about the cover

Our survey findings reveal the persistent effects of partisanship, racial identification, news attentiveness, and ideology on evaluation of the caricature. Table 2 provides results from an analysis of variance (ANOVA) analysis of the Pew Data comparing the mean differences in perceptions about the cover. Whites were more likely to endorse publication of the caricature than were non-Whites. Whites were also less likely to think the cover was offensive or racist. As expected, Democrats uniformly differed from Republicans on the evaluative measures. Democrats were nearly twice as likely as were Republicans to view the cover as unfunny, oppose publication, and dismiss the caricature as being clever. Republicans were less likely than counterparts to call the caricature racist.

Table 3 displays the binary logistic regression results for whether respondents viewed the caricature as offensive, racist, funny, or clever. Consistent with findings from the ANOVA analysis, Democrats were significantly more likely to see the caricature as offensive even after controlling for gender, education, and income. The average marginal effect of being a Democrat on the probability of seeing the cover as "offensive" was an 18 percentage-point increase. Respondents who reported that they most closely followed news about Afghanistan were less likely to label the caricature as offensive. Shifting from following other stories to following news about Afghanistan lowered the probability of calling the caricature offensive by 21 percentage points. On the other hand, these respondents were not more or less likely

Table 3. Logistic Regression Estimates for News Attentiveness Model Predicting Response to the "Politics of Fear" *New Yorker* Cover (Pew Data).

	DV = answered "yes" that word below described cover			
Variable	Offensive	Racist	Clever	Funny
Black	0.315	0.417	0.333	− 0.383
Other racial minority	− 0.0198	0.353	− 0.678	− 0.457
Latino	0.211	− 0.545	− 0.105	0.140
Democrat	0.809**	0.618*	− 0.816**	− 0.704*
Republican	− 0.116	− 0.788*	− 0.305	− 0.274
Female	0.260	0.302	− 0.464	− 0.914***
Income	− 0.183	− 0.0695	0.0176	− 0.0008
Education	0.0183	− 0.230**	0.155	− 0.0972
Age	0.0990*	0.0580	− 0.0733	− 0.0350
News: Followed Iraq	0.574	0.708	− 0.573	− 0.0896
News: Followed Afghanistan	− 0.964*	− 0.554	0.664	1.555***
News: Obama more favorable	0.0763	0.239	− 1.092**	0.123
News: Obama less favorable	− 0.0429	− 0.222	0.422	0.415
Resides in Center City	0.0428	− 0.0942	− 0.0149	0.0424
Constant	− 0.546	0.110	− 0.182	0.294
Observations	421	420	418	422

Note. DV = dependent variable. STATA 14 used for equations. *Source*: News Interest Index Omnibus Survey, July 18–21, 2008 (Weighted Data). Excluded baseline categories are White and Independent.
*p < .05. **p < .01. ***p < .001.

Table 4. Multinomial Logistic Regression Estimates for Impact of News Attentiveness and Social Demography on Selection of Statement about What Was Conveyed by *The New Yorker* 'Politics of Fear' Caricature.

	Muslim		Radical		Violent		Un-American	
Variable	B	SE	B	SE	B	SE	B	SE
Female	0.281	(0.216)	0.144	(0.241)	0.431†	(0.253)	− 0.0889	(0.171)
Democrat	− 1.291***	(0.377)	− 0.229	(0.428)	− 0.314	(0.462)	− 0.501	(0.304)
Republican	− 1.125***	(0.327)	− 0.425	(0.365)	0.345	(0.389)	− 0.0167	(0.256)
Obama voter	− 0.0498	(0.369)	− 1.304**	(0.445)	− 0.147	(0.451)	− 0.657*	(0.315)
White	0.189	(0.549)	0.876	(0.586)	− 0.0967	(0.545)	0.307	(0.369)
Black	0.196	(0.701)	− 0.785	(1.195)	0.263	(0.652)	0.436	(0.472)
Latino	1.126	(0.712)	1.307†	(0.762)	0.409	(0.741)	1.153*	(0.513)
Religiosity	0.0405	(0.0276)	0.0165	(0.0291)	0.0315	(0.0313)	0.0141	(0.0194)
News interest	0.369†	(0.193)	0.305	(0.214)	0.0635	(0.213)	0.128	(0.166)
Warmth toward Blacks	− 0.00584	(0.00589)	− 0.00906	(0.00578)	− 0.00698	(0.00624)	− 0.00371	(0.00455)
Iraq mistake	− 0.157	(0.127)	− 0.0858	(0.170)	− 0.235	(0.156)	− 0.0129	(0.103)
Family income	0.0119	(0.0355)	− 0.00602	(0.0399)	− 0.0327	(0.0368)	0.0195	(0.0272)
Liberal	0.0241	(0.320)	0.564	(0.356)	− 0.333	(0.359)	0.294	(0.228)
Conservative	− 0.137	(0.336)	0.427	(0.388)	0.416	(0.401)	0.283	(0.270)
Age	− 0.0927	(0.153)	0.00742	(0.187)	− 0.302†	(0.178)	− 0.144	(0.125)
Education	− 0.302***	(0.0817)	− 0.0767	(0.0922)	− 0.0984	(0.0965)	− 0.139*	(0.0608)
Confederate South	− 0.343	(0.245)	− 0.0131	(0.269)	− 0.175	(0.275)	− 0.300	(0.181)
Constant	1.132	(1.112)	− 0.751	(1.099)	0.687	(1.049)	1.231	(0.811)
Observations	1,169							

Notes. STATA 14 used for equations. Reference category is "Image Conveys None" and excluded categories are independent, other minority, and moderate. *Source*. 2008 Cooperative Congressional Election Study (weighted data).
†p < .10. *p < .05. **p < .01. ***p < .001.

to see the cover as racist. High levels of education were associated with a decreased likelihood to see the caricature as racist. On average, moving from the lowest level to the highest level of the educational attainment scale decreased the probability by 28.5 percentage points. The effects of education and news attentiveness disappear and reemerge, respectively, in the last two columns. Respondents holding a "more favorable opinion of Obama" were less likely than those with "no change in opinion" to see the cover as clever.

To further explore public perceptions of the "Politics of Fear" caricature, we examined descriptive statistics from the 2008 CCES task where respondents were asked to select one of five statements. Overall, 27% of respondents selected that "the image conveys none of these [four] statements." Nearly 38% choose "the Obamas are un-American," and nearly 18% choose "Barack Obama is a Muslim." This latter statistic is higher than the 13% of people found in 2008 national surveys who believed Barack was a Muslim, and lower than the 29% of people holding a similar view by 2015. Although 36% of Democrats selected the "conveys none" statement, 28% of Republicans and 18% of Independents selected this option. As hypothesized, supporters of Obama had a different selection pattern than non-supporters, with the former being less likely to select the statement that the Obamas were un-American. Nonsupporters were less likely to be conflicted about what statement the cover may have conveyed. There was no significant difference in the likelihood of nonsupporters and supporters choosing the "Barack is a Muslim" statement. Consistent with the Pew Data, news attentiveness helped to shape selection. The most attentive were less likely to choose the first three derogatory statements.

Results from the multinomial logistic regression of the CCES Data are displayed in Table 4. These mirror patterns seen in the ANOVA and binary logistic regression results from the Pew Data. Partisan affiliation significantly predicted whether a respondent choose the "Conveys None" (baseline condition) over the "Muslim" statement, with Republicans and Democrats more likely to select the former. Education was a significant predictor as to whether a respondent selected the former over the latter, with higher levels of education leading to greater aversion to the "Muslim" statement. The reversals in the effect of partisan identification for choosing the other three statements relative to the baseline provide further confirmation that the images within *The New Yorker* cover had become most associated with a narrative that the Obamas were un-American. As discussed above, before the appearance of *The New Yorker* cover, the "Obama is a Muslim" narrative became partially subsumed, but not totally integrated, into discussions on Barack's fit for the Oval Office and on the couple's un-American/anti-Americanness. As shown in Column 4 and Column 8, Obama supporters were significantly less likely to choose the "radical" statement and the "un-American" statement relative to the baseline. Having reported to have voted for Obama decreased the probability of selecting the former by eight percent, and increased the probability of selecting the baseline by 10%. Compared to others, Latinos saw the image as suggestive that the Obamas were un-American.

Table 5. Differences in Probabilities of Hypothetical Young White Republican and Democratic Constituent Selecting Each Statement by Level of News Attentiveness.

Statement	Most of the time	Some of the time	Only now and then	Hardly at all
Barack is a Muslim				
Democrat	0.121	0.154	0.192	0.236
Republican	0.059	0.075	0.094	0.116
Difference	0.062	0.079	0.098	0.120
Michelle is a radical				
Democrat	0.079	0.094	0.110	0.127
Republican	0.096	0.114	0.134	0.156
Difference	−0.017	−0.020	−0.024	−0.029
Obamas are violent				
Democrat	0.065	0.061	0.057	0.051
Republican	0.144	0.134	0.124	0.113
Difference	−0.079	−0.073	−0.067	−0.062
Obamas are un-American				
Democrat	0.371	0.371	0.364	0.351
Republican	0.532	0.529	0.521	0.506
Difference	−0.161	−0.158	−0.157	−0.155
Image conveys none of the above statements				
Democrat	0.364	0.320	0.277	0.235
Republican	0.169	0.148	0.128	0.109
Difference	0.195	0.172	0.149	0.12

Notes. STATA 14 used for equations. Probabilities derived from results of multinomial logistic regression where race is set to white, party is set to Democrat or Republican, age is set to the 18–34 category, ideology is set to liberal or conservative, 2008 presidential vote is set to Obama or Not Obama, and the remaining variables are set to their means. *Source.* 2008 Cooperative Congressional Election Study.

To gain better leverage on the cumulative effects of the aforementioned variables, we generated two predicted probability profiles derived from the multinomial estimates in Table 4. For the first profile, we set race to White, party to Democrat, age to 18–34, ideology to liberal, vote choice to Obama, and set the remaining variables to their sample means. For the second profile, we set race to White, age to 18–34, party to Republican, ideology to conservative, vote choice to not Obama, and left the remaining variables at their sample means. These two profiles serve as proxies for the young, White, partisan ideologues who were typical Obama and McCain supporters (Crotty, 2009). Next, we calculated probability differences by news attentiveness. Table 5 reports these results. At the highest end of the news attentiveness scale, there was a 20% difference in the probability of each profile selecting the baseline condition. Also, the hypothetical Republican had a 16% higher predicted probability of selecting the "un-American" statement regardless of news attentiveness. At the lowest end of the news attentiveness scale, Republicans had a higher probability of selecting the "radical" or "violent" statement. In other words, the hypothetical Democrat was predicted to mostly avoid the derogatory statements, whereas the hypothetical Republican was predicted to mostly avoid the baseline statement.

Discussion

As a visual communicative device, *The New Yorker* cover unified disparate trepidations about the Obamas. Our results suggest however that the visual resonated with those most likely to oppose Barack's bid for the Presidency even though many Republican elites did denounce the caricature (Joseph, 2011). Many, however, did not see it as caricature assassination. Soon other outlets parodied *The New Yorker*'s attempt to ridicule anti-Obama rhetoric, including mass publications such as *Vanity Fair, The Nation, Entertainment Weekly, National Review*, among others (Linkins, 2008; *Vanity Fair*, 2008; Vanden Heuvel, 2008; Wolk, 2008). This media frenzy assured that the caricature, but not necessarily the underlying joke, went beyond *The New Yorker*'s high-end readership.

The *New Yorker* published two other covers seemingly inspired by Blitt's caricature. The first featured Barack and Santa Claus in a parody of the former bowing to the Japanese emperor in 2009; the second parodied House Speaker John Boehner's failed attempt to fist bump with Obama in 2010 (Mouly & Flanangin, 2012). Those parodying the original caricature presumed that the mass public could appreciate the folly of fetishizing a candidate's identities. However, as Wingfield and Feagin (2009) noted, no article within the July edition provided an interpretative framework to understand the joke. Moreover, neither the illustrator nor the editor of *The New Yorker* could control how the caricature was received or exploited. Senator Obama was not confident that Americans outside *The New Yorker*'s readership would get the pro-Obama satire of anti-Obama rhetoric, or that the satire would shame the anti-Obama activists. Our results and the results of others suggest that Obama was correct (Rossing, 2011).

Our iconographical analysis revealed a heavy reliance on "Barack is a Muslim" and "the Obamas are un-American" motifs. By using the Oval Office as a backdrop, Blitt's caricature connected trepidations that the Obamas would use the White House, both a private familial space and taxpayer-funded public space, for anti-American behavior. By depicting Michelle as an afro-wearing, gun-toting, camouflage-wearing radical, Blitt portrayed Michelle in a state of violent readiness and forever linked her with recognizable symbols of the Black Panther Party, an organization that rejected White hegemony and preached Black pride. Blitt's caricature played to the racialized, gendered, and xenophobic narratives trafficked during the 2008 election cycle: that the Obamas were deceitful and foreign to White Americans.

By the spring of 2016, all evidence suggested that the Obamas were never able to fully dispel White belief in or exploitation of these narratives. These narratives were front and center during the 2008 and 2012 Republican presidential rallies. Video of McCain supporters saying Obama is "Arab" at a 2008 town hall meeting went viral during that election cycle, and McCain's disagreement and insistence that Obama was a "descent family man" and a "citizen" fueled internal party debates about whether McCain was conservative and hardnosed enough for Republican voters. The Birther Movement and the Tea Party Movement trafficked in the "Obama is anti-/un-American" narratives in 2010, 2012, and 2014 to retain and strengthen Republican congressional majorities. By the 2016 cycle, Republican elites, some with presidential aspirations, were exploiting the narratives to galvanize White anger (Healy, 2015). For example, an attendee at a 2015 rally for Republican presidential hopeful Donald Trump reportedly yelled that Obama was "a Muslim" and "not ... American" (Johnson, 2015, para 1). Sidestepping her role in perpetuating the 2008 "Barack is a Muslim" narrative, 2016 Democratic presidential hopeful Hillary Clinton took to Twitter to rebuke Trump for "not denouncing false statements about POTUS" (Clinton, 2015; MacAskill, 2008). Our results from the 2008 CCES survey data show that these narratives were cemented before 2016. In fact, a 2015 CNN/ORC poll showed that almost thirty percent of polled Americans believe that Obama was Muslim, a number that had doubled since 2008 and 2012 (Agiesta, 2015; Pew, 2008b, 2012). Fifty-four percent of polled Trump supporters and forty-three percent of Republicans shared that sentiment (Agiesta, 2015). However, 60% of college degree holders thought Obama was a Protestant (Agiesta, 2015). Our survey findings show a similar pattern: Party, news interest, and education correlated with whether one choose the "Barack is a Muslim" theme.

Conclusion

The "Politics of Fear" caricature on the cover of the July 2008 *New Yorker* magazine was typical and atypical amongst anti-Obama visual and rhetorical communications during the 2008 campaign (Joseph, 2011). Such communications highlighted White anxiety about race and power; and the Internet guaranteed world-wide dissemination of each anti-Obama text. The illustrator claimed the caricature was satire of anti-Barack and Michelle narratives, or an attempt at caricature assassination. However, our mixed method analysis revealed the satire may have missed its mark. The caricature amplified the currency of sexist, racialized, xenophobic anxiety about an Obama Presidency. The technicolor caricature created a visually arresting image by superimposing concerns about the Obamas' Americanness onto themselves. As a satirical product, however, neither the caricature nor its viewers could easily escape the racism that the caricature trafficked in. Our survey findings of racial, partisan, and ideological differences in responses to *The New Yorker* cover parallel findings using newspaper and rhetoric analysis to examine the caricature (Joseph, 2011; Rossing, 2011).

In conclusion, our research advanced the study of visual communication by further integrating visual and survey analyses. We also documented why Black subjects of political caricatures are at greater risk for being negatively affected than satirists are at risk for being under appreciated. Because visual communication shapes public attitudes (Johnson, Dolan, & Sonnett, 2011), particular images in particular contexts can enhance voter reliance on heuristic devices which presumably signal a candidate's acumen and allegiances (Becker & Haller, 2014; Schwartz, 2011). *The New Yorker* cover therefore may have unknowingly enhanced, rather than displaced, suspicions amongst Whites that the Obamas were ill-suited for the White House. Although Michelle Obama stated the cover was satire in 2015, the caricature was emotionally unsettling to her and she remembers it (incorrectly) as her first appearance on any magazine (The White House, Office of the First Lady, 2015). That White summations of the Obama Presidency often draw upon the anti-/un-American narratives undermine the legitimacy of claims about a post-racial America.

Note

1. Supplemental materials are available at http://www.elkastevens.com/TechnicolorRacism.pdf.

References

Agiesta, J. (2015, Sept 14). *Misperceptions persist about Obama's faith, but aren't so widespread.* Retrieved from http://www.cnn.com/2015/09/13/politics/barack-obama-religion-christian-misperceptions/

Ansolabehere, S. (2009). *Guide to the 2010 Cooperative Congressional Election Survey.* Cambridge, MA: Harvard University. Retrieved from http://projects.iq.harvard.edu/cces/book/study-design

Associated Press. (2006, August 17). *Obama travels to Africa for 5-nation tour: Hopes for special resonance as senator, son of Kenyan goat herder.* Retrieved from http://www.msnbc.msn.com/id/14391213/

Banaji, M. R. (2008, August 1). The science of satire: Cognition studies clash with *New Yorker* rationale. *The Chronicle of Higher Education, 54.* Retrieved from http://chronicle.com/article/The-Science-of-Satire/20523

Bates, B. R., Lawrence, W., & Cervenka, M. (2008). Redrawing Afrocentrism: Visual *Nommo* in George H. ben Johnson's editorial cartoons. *Howard Journal of Communications, 25,* 34–55. http://dx.doi.org/10.1080/10646170802225219

Beam, C. (2008, June 10). *Pounds* [Web blog post]. Retrieved from http://www.slate.com/blogs/blogs/trailhead/archive/2008/06/04/pounds.aspx

Becker, A. B., & Haller, B. A. (2014). When political comedy turns personal: Humor types, audience evaluations, and attitudes. *Howard Journal of Communications, 25,* 34–55. http://dx.doi.org/10.1080/10646175.2013.835607

Beinart, P. (2008, October 9). Is Barack Obama American enough? *Time.* Retrieved from http://www.time.com/time/magazine/article/0,9171,1848755,00.html

Bell, P. (2005). Content analysis of visual images. In T. van Leeuwen & C. Jewitt, (Eds.), *The handbook of visual analysis* (pp. 10–34). Thousand Oaks, CA: SAGE.

Blitt, B. (2008, July 21). The politics of fear [Illustration]. *The New Yorker.* Retrieved from http://www.newyorker.com/images/covers/2008/2008_07_21_p323.jpg

Caricature. (2010). In *Merriam Webster's online dictionary.* Retrieved from http://www.merriam-webster.com/dictionary/caricature

Clayton, D. (2010). *The presidential campaign of Barack Obama: A critical analysis of a racially transcendent strategy.* New York, NY: Routledge.

Clinton, H. (2015, Sept 17). *Donald Trump not denouncing false statements about POTUS & hateful rhetoric about Muslims is disturbing, & just plain wrong. Cut it out. -H.* [Tweet]. Retrieved from https://twitter.com/HillaryClinton/status/644710016633712640

Condé Nast. (2009). The New Yorker *Circulation/Demographics* [Media kit]. Retrieved from http://www.condenast.com/brands/new-yorker/media-kit/print

Condé Nast Collection. (2016). *The New Yorker* Cover—July 21, 2008. [Online store]. Retrieved from http://www.condenaststore.com/-sp/The-New-Yorker-Cover-July-21-2008-Prints_i8482992_.htm

Conners, J. L. (2005). Visual representations of the 2004 presidential campaign: Political cartoons and popular culture references. *American Behavioral Scientist, 49,* 479–487.

Crotty, W. (2009). Electing Obama: The 2008 presidential campaign. In W. Crotty (Ed.), *Winning the presidency 2008* (pp. 20–47). Boulder, CO: Paradigm Publishers.

El Refaie, E. (2009). Multiliteracies: How readers interpret political cartoons. *Visual Communication, 8*(1), 181–205.

Harris-Perry, M. V. (2011). *Sister citizen: Shame, stereotypes, and black women in America*. New Haven, CT: Yale University Press.

Healy, P. (2015, September 18). Willing to spend $100 million, Donald Trump has so far reveled in free publicity. *New York Times*. Retrieved from http://www.nytimes.com/2015/09/19/us/politics/donald-trump-republican-nomination.html?_r=1

Hillestad, R. (1980). The underlying structure of appearance. *Dress, 6*, 117–125.

Johnson, J. (2015, September 17). Trump doesn't correct rally attendee who says Obama is Muslim and "not even an American." *Washington Post*. Retrieved from https://www.washingtonpost.com/news/post-politics/wp/2015/09/17/trump-doesnt-correct-rally-attendee-who-says-obama-is-muslim-and-not-even-an-american/

Johnson, K. A., Dolan, M. K., & Sonnett, J. (2011). Speaking of Looting: An analysis of racial propaganda in national television coverage of Hurricane Katrina. *Howard Journal of Communications, 22*, 302–318.

Johnson, S., & Prijatel, P. (2000). *Magazine publishing*. Lincolnwood, IL: NTC/Contemporary Publishing Group.

Joseph, R. L. (2011). Imagining Obama: Reading overtly and inferentially racist images of our 44th President, 2007–2008. *Communication Studies, 62*, 389–405. http://dx.doi.org/10.1080/10510974.2011.588074

Kelly, K. J. (2008, July 25). Barack sells out. *New York Post*. Retrieved from http://nypost.com/2008/07/25/barack-obama-sells-out/

King-Meadows, T. (2008). *Cooperative Congressional Election Study, 2008: UMBC/NCOBPS Module* [Computer File]. Baltimore, MD: University of Maryland Baltimore County.

Linkins, J. (2008, July 15). A *New Yorker* cover for *National Review*. Retrieved from http://www.huffingtonpost.com/2008/07/15/a-new-yorker-cover-for-na_n_112877.html

MacAskill, E. (2008, February 28). *Clinton aides claim Obama photo not intended as a smear*. Retrieved from http://www.theguardian.com/world/2008/feb/25/barackobama.hillaryclinton

Marshall, G. (1998). *Bogardus Social Distance Scale*. Retrieved from http://www.encyclopedia.com/doc/1O88-Bogardussocialdistancescl.html

McShane, L. (2008, June 6). Barack and Michelle Obama's 'fist bump of hope' shows them silly in love. *New York Daily News*. Retrieved from http://www.nydailynews.com/news/politics/2008/06/05/2008-06-05_barack_and_michelle_obamas_fist_bump_of_.html

Mitchell, M. (2008, June 19). Michelle Obama bitter? Not likely. *Chicago Sun Times*. Retrieved from http://www.suntimes.com/news/mitchell/1013609,CST-NWS-mitch19.article

Mooney, A. (2008, July 14). *New Yorker* editor defends controversial Obama cover. *CNN.com*. Retrieved from http://www.cnn.com/2008/POLITICS/07/14/obama.cover/index.html

Mouly, F., & Flanagin, J. (2012, June 28). Cover story: Obama moments. *The New Yorker*. Retrieved from http://www.newyorker.com/culture/culture-desk/cover-story-obama-moments

Müller, M. G., & Özcan, E. (2007). The political iconography of Muhammad cartoons: Understanding cultural conflict and political action. *PS: Political Science & Politics, 40*, 287–291.

National Public Radio. (2008, February 25). *Pics of Obama in Muslim garb circulated on web* [News blog]. Retrieved from http://www.npr.org/blogs/news/2008/02/pics_of_obama_in_muslim_garb_c.html

Norris, M. (Host). (2008, July 14). *New Yorker* editor defends Obama cover [Radio broadcast transcript]. *All Things Considered*. Washington, DC: National Public Radio. Retrieved from http://www.npr.org/templates/transcript/transcript.php?storyId=92529393

Panofsky, E. (1972). *Studies in iconology humanistic themes in the art of the Renaissance.* Boulder, CO: Westview Press.

Parlett, M. A. (2014). *Demonizing a president: The "foreignization" of Barack Obama.* Santa Barabra, CA: Praeger.

Pew Research Center. (2008a, September 18). *McCain gains on issues, but stalls as candidate of change.* Retrieved from http://people-press.org/report/450/presidential-race-remains-even

Pew Research Center. (2008b, May 1). *Obama's image slips, his lead over Clinton disappears.* Retrieved from http://people-press.org/report/414/obamas-image-slips-his-lead-over-clinton-disappears

Pew Research Center. (2009). Magazines. In *The state of the news media 2009: An annual report on American journalism.* Retrieved from http://www.stateofthemedia.org/2009/narrative_magazines_audience.php?media=9&cat=2

Pitney, N. (2008, July 13). Barry Blitt defends his *New Yorker* cover art of Obama. *The Huffington Post.* Retrieved from http://www.huffingtonpost.com/2008/07/13/barry-blitt-addresses-his_n_112432.html

Powell, M. (2008, February 25). Photo of Obama in African garb emerges as Clinton renews attacks. *The New York Times.* Retrieved from http://www.nytimes.com/2008/02/25/world/americas/25iht-25webcamp.10383545.html

Powell, M., & Kantor, J. (2008, June 18). After attacks, Michelle Obama looks for a new introduction. *The New York Times.* Retrieved from http://www.nytimes.com/2008/06/18/us/politics/18michelle.html

Roach-Higgins, M., & Eicher, J. (1992). Dress and identity. *Clothing and Textiles Research Journal, 10*(4), 1–8.

Rossing, J. P. (2011). Comic provocations in racial culture: Barack Obama and the "Politics of Fear." *Communication Studies, 62,* 422–438.

Schwartz, J. (2011). Framing Power: Comparing U.S. newspaper visuals of Latino and non-Latino candidates. *Howard Journal of Communications, 22,* 377–393.

Simien, E. M. (2016). *Historic firsts: How symbolic empowerment changes U.S. politics.* New York, NY: Oxford.

Stephey, M. J. (2008, June 5). A brief history of the fist bump. *Time.* Retrieved from http://content.time.com/time/nation/article/0,8599,1812102,00.html

Texas v. Johnson, 491 U.S. 397 (1989).

The New Yorker. (2008, July 13). In this week's *New Yorker*: How Chicago shaped Obama [Press Release]. Retrieved from http://www.newyorker.com/services/presscenter/2008/07/21/080721pr_press_releases?printable=true#ixzz0qJ5tisg1

The New Yorker. (2009). About us. Retrieved from http://www.newyorker.com/about/us/

The White House, Office of the First Lady. (2015, May 9). *Remarks by the First Lady at Tuskegee University commencement address* [Speech]. Retrieved from https://www.whitehouse.gov/the-press-office/2015/05/09/remarks-first-lady-tuskegee-university-commencement-address

Traub, J. (2007, November 4). Is (his) biography (our) destiny. *New York Times Magazine.* Retrieved from http://www.nytimes.com/2007/11/04/magazine/04obama-t.html

Tristam, P. (2008, July 14). *Satire or slander?* The New Yorker's *Obama Mujahideen* [Pierre's Middle East issues blog]. Retrieved from http://middleeast.about.com/b/2008/07/14/satire-or-slander-the-new-yorkers-obama-mujahideens.htm

United States Code (4 U.S. Code 1). Retrieved from https://www.gpo.gov/fdsys/pkg/USCODE-2011-title4/html/USCODE-2011-title4-chap1.htm

United States v. Eichman, 496 US 310 Supreme Court (1990).

Vanden Heuvel, K. (2008). *The New Yorker* Controversy. *The Nation.* Retrieved from http://www.ew.com/ew/article/0,,20228603,00.html

Vanity Fair. (2008, July 22). *Vanity Fair* covers *The New Yorker*. Retrieved from http://www.vanityfair.com/online/daily/2008/07/new-yorker-cover.html

van Leeuwen, T. (2005). Semiotics and iconography. In T. van Leeuwen & C. Jewitt, (Eds.), *The handbook of visual analysis* (pp. 92–119). Thousand Oaks, CA: Sage.

van Leeuwen, T. & Jewitt, C. (2005). Introduction. In T. van Leeuwen & C. Jewitt, (Eds.), *The handbook of visual analysis* (pp. 14–15). Thousand Oaks, CA: Sage.

Wallace, J. (Executive Producer). (2008, June 6). *America's pulse* [Television broadcast]. New York, NY: Fox News. Retrieved from http://mediamatters.org/mmtv/200806060007

Waters, H. (Producer). (2008, July 15). *Larry King live!* [Television broadcast]. Atlanta, GA: Cable News Network.

Wingfield, A. H., & Feagin, J. R. (2009). *Yes we can? White racial framing and the 2008 Presidential campaign*. New York, NY: Routledge.

Wolk, J. (2008, September 30). *Jon Stewart and Stephen Colbert: Mock the vote*. Retrieved from http://www.ew.com/ew/article/0,,20228603,00.html

State of Nations: Barack Obama's Indigenous America

R. E. Glenn

> **ABSTRACT**
> From his "adoption" by a Crow Nation family while on the campaign trail in 2008, to his renaming of Mt. McKinley to Denali—the mountain's Koyukon Athabascan name—Barack Obama has enjoyed a relationship with Indigenous Americans that is unique in presidential history. He has spent more time in "Indian country," as it is officially known by the federal government, than any other president. Moreover, he has implemented an annual Tribal Nations Conference to facilitate consultation between the federal government and Indigenous leadership. In this article, the author argues that Obama's discourse of Indigenous issues is marked by a particular form of rhetoric, constitutive rhetoric, through which he calls into existence a new, inclusive relationship between the United States and tribal governments. Focusing primarily on his speeches at Tribal Nations Conferences, the author identifies a "nations-within" concept adhered to by Obama that contrasts markedly with past presidential rhetoric concerning Indigenous Americans.

In May of 2008, Representative Diane Watson was not particularly happy with Senator Barack Obama, a candidate in the race for the Democratic presidential nomination. Watson and other members of the Congressional Black Caucus had recently introduced House Resolution 2824, a bill proposing to punitively sever the federal government's relationship with the Cherokee Nation of Oklahoma. The tribe had recently held a referendum vote to limit tribal membership to people who could trace their ancestry to signers of the Dawes Rolls of Cherokees, a census of the tribe taken by the federal government in 1906. The referendum effectively excluded "Freedmen," descendants of non-Cherokee African Americans who had been listed on a separate Cherokee Freedmen Rolls, also taken in 1906.

Candidate Obama, despite being touted as, potentially, the first African American president, had publicly expressed his opposition to H.R. 2824. Watson saw Obama's opposition to her proposed legislation as an affront to the long history of civil rights expansion that would eventually culminate in his own election to the presidency. Senator Obama, however, believed that the Cherokees' vote on tribal membership was an issue of tribal sovereignty (Watson, 2008).

The Cherokee referendum to limit tribal membership to Cherokees-by-blood and Watson's subsequent punitive legislation were the most recent vestiges of a federal policy of Indigenous assimilation that began in the late 19th century and continued through much of the 20th. The federal government had created the Dawes Rolls, named for Massachusetts Senator Henry Dawes, an ardent assimilationist. The census rolls were designed to individualize tribal members from their collective societies. Once the rolls were taken, each tribal member was issued a tract of land, with hopes that he or she would become a Euro American-style agrarian. The Freedmen, however, posed a problem to the federal roll-takers of the early 20th century. They weren't Indigenous, but they had been deemed citizens of the Cherokee Nation in the Treaty of 1866. That treaty forced the Cherokee Nation, which had included slave owners and had fought with the South in the Civil War, to extend citizenship to emancipated slaves of Cherokees. The roll-takers resolved the issue by simply creating a different list—the Cherokee Freedmen Rolls.

In the 21st century, descendants of the Freedmen have argued that, under the Treaty of 1866, they still deserve Cherokee tribal membership. The Cherokee Nation has contended that tribal sovereignty includes the ability to determine tribal membership, and that Cherokee citizenship belongs only to Cherokees-by-blood. The ethical ramifications of the Cherokees' exclusion of the Freedmen from tribal membership have been discussed at length elsewhere (Sturm, 2002), and the issue currently remains unresolved. That an African American presidential candidate saw the Freedmen issue—not as one of African American civil rights—but rather, as one of tribal sovereignty, was a harbinger to tribal leaders across the nation that a new era of United States/Indigenous relations could be on the political horizon.

In fact, the Obama presidency may well mark a watershed moment in such relations. It stands as a potential turning point, depending on the policies of subsequent administrations, toward the sorts of relations Indigenous critical scholars and tribal leaders alike have been imploring the federal government to facilitate for decades. Lakota scholar Vine Deloria wrote his Indian manifesto, *Custer Died for Your Sins* (1969), in the midst of the civil rights struggles of the 1960s. He pointed out that many Americans tended to view the Indigenous peoples of the American continent as yet one more minority group facing the same obstacles of systemic racism and lack of opportunity as many others. But Indigenes' demands on American society and governance are significantly different. They already had social and governmental structures in place long before the European colonization of the Americas. They were already nations and would like to retain many aspects of those precolonization systems. Rather than working to gain access to the American Dream, as other marginalized groups were doing, Indigenous Americans were often trying to disentangle themselves from it (Deloria, 1969, Chapter 8). As Deloria quite vituperatively put it,

> The most common attitude Indians have faced has been the unthoughtful Johnny-come-lately liberal who equates certain goals with a dark skin. This type of individual generally defines the goals of all groups by the way he understands what he wants for blacks. (p. 170)

Deloria, the foremost Indigenous scholar of the 20th century (Lake, 1983), died in 2005. But, given the tenor of the above passage, he likely would have appreciated the irony in the fact that the first American president to host an annual Tribal Nations Conference, and to be referred to, only half-jokingly, by an Indigenous American tribal leader as "the first American Indian president," would, in fact, be the first African American president, Barack Obama (Sink, 2012).

In this article, I examine the presidential rhetoric of Barack Obama—both his words and actions—as it relates to the more than five-hundred Indigenous tribes that currently exist in the United States. I focus predominantly on President Obama's speeches to the annual Tribal Nations Conferences that he hosted each year of his presidency in Washington, DC. I undertake this examination through the lens of constitutive rhetoric, discourse that calls into being a collective identity, that constructs "the people" that are its very subjects (McGee, 1975). I argue that Obama's presidential rhetoric presents America, not as a nation of states, as our national title, The United States of America, would suggest, but rather as a state of nations. He rhetorically constructs a nation of disparate identities that, despite their differences, contribute to a broader American ethos while still retaining indigenous national identities. To support this argument, I will first examine two key terms, *sovereign* and *nation*, as they relate to Indigenous American tribes. Second, I will demonstrate how Obama's presidential rhetoric has not only respected, but adhered to, the Indigenous reading of those terms, while at the same time presenting the United States as a plurality of nations. Finally, I will conclude with implications of President Obama's rhetorical constitution of the people he called "the first Americans" (Obama, 2009). As I will demonstrate, for many Americans, Barack Obama's most enduring legacy may be his recognition that they are more than Americans. They are also members of nations that existed long before Euro-Americans came to this continent, and they are welcome to retain those indigenous national identities.

Conceding the contested nature of the terms *nation* and *state*, not to mention the hyphenated combination thereof, I follow what I believe are the least confusing usages of the terms (Tishkov, 2000, p. 627). By "nation-state," I am designating a geo-political entity that enjoys widely recognized sovereignty—yet another contested term—such as the United States, France, Kenya, and Japan. In the following section, *nation* and *sovereignty* will, despite their slippery nature, become more clearly defined, if only for the duration of this article.

Indigenous sovereign nations

When Barack Obama drew the ire of Rep. Diane Watson by describing the Cherokee Freedmen controversy as a sovereignty issue, he was implementing one of two terms that have framed United States/Indigenous relations for almost two centuries—*sovereignty* and *nation*. Both terms make ample appearance in a series of Supreme Court decisions issued in the 1830s, when the executive branch under President Andrew Jackson was attempting to remove Indigenous tribes from the eastern seaboard states to areas west of the Mississippi River. Although the decisions specifically addressed the Cherokee Nation, they applied more broadly to all Indigenous peoples living in the regions claimed by the United States at that time. In those decisions, Chief Justice John Marshall set forth the language that would come to serve as a template for United States/Indigenous relations for the rest of the 19th century. It was a template, however, that contained significant ambiguity.

Marshall wrote in *Cherokee Nation v. Georgia* (1831) that the Indigenous peoples in the United States were "domestic dependent nations," who "look to our government for protection; rely upon its kindness and its power; appeal to it for relief to their wants," and were "completely under the sovereignty and dominion of the United States" (Sec. 18–19). He stopped short of allowing Indigenous tribes the same sovereignty as enjoyed by the United States and European nations:

> The Indian nations had always been considered as distinct, independent political communities, retaining their original natural rights, as the undisputed possessors of the soil, from time immemorial, with the single exception of that imposed by irresistible power, which excluded them from intercourse with any other European potentate than the first discoverer of the coast of the particular region claimed. (*Worcester v. Georgia*, 1832, Section 186)

Sovereignty is a term that has been considered for millennia, with the first known mention of the concept appearing in the writings of the 5th century BCE Greek poet Pindarus. In Fragment 169, Pindarus equated sovereignty with *nomos*, or law (Agamben, 1998). It is, he contended, the defining characteristic of the entity who "rules with the strongest hand, justifying the most violent." More recently, Georgio Agamben (1998) drew on the Pindarian conception of sovereignty as the potential for legal violence, along with Carl Schmitt's position (1974) that sovereignty belongs to the entity who determines exception to law (p. 67). Agamben concluded that sovereignty is nothing more than a veiled exhibition of the same tendencies that exist in nature, or domination by the strongest and most violent (Agamben, Chapter 2).

All three readings of sovereignty—offered by Pindarus, Schmitt, and Agamben—appear to be applicable to Chief Justice John Marshall's 1831 decision in *Cherokee Nation v. Georgia*. Drawing on a most Schmittian conception of exception, Marshall wrote that, "[t]he condition of the Indians in relation to the United States is perhaps unlike that of any other two people in existence," (Section 16). In an exercise of U.S government sovereignty itself, Marshall declared the exception: Indigenous tribes were "domestic dependent(s)" of the United States. However, 1 year later, in *Worcester v. Georgia* (1832), he described them as "distinct, independent political communities" or "nations" (Section 186). Marshall defined *nation* as "a people distinct from others" (Ibid). In sum, Indigenous tribes were, according to Marshall, nations without sovereignty. They lacked the potential for violence, or the "irresistible power," in this case, of the United States, referenced in the above extended quotation. It was this very power that Pindarus considered a presupposition of sovereignty. Yet, according to Marshall, tribes still retained nationalistic qualities that necessitated treaty-signing between themselves and the United States.

Marshall's view of Indigenous Americans, as expressed in the Cherokee Nation cases, remained the dominant understanding of United States/Indigenous relations until the end of the nineteenth century. The federal government ceased treaty-signing with tribal nations in 1871. Shortly thereafter, the aforementioned assimilation program using the Dawes Rolls as a mechanism to individualize members of every tribe in the United States from their respective collectivistic tribal identities effectively ended any nationalism still remaining among the Indigenous peoples of the United States. In the 20th century, however, Congress passed reorganization acts that allowed some degree of national reconstitution by tribes. The Indian Reorganization Act of 1934 and the Oklahoma Indian Welfare Act of 1936 allowed descendants of signers of the Dawes Rolls to form corporations, bearing the names of their respective tribal identities and charged with improving conditions for corporate-tribal members. To this day, many of those corporatized tribes refer to their executive leaders as "chairmen," rather than the more traditional "chief." In addition, the Principal Chiefs Act of 1970 gave the most populous tribes in Oklahoma—the Cherokee, Choctaw, Creek, and Seminole—the power to reform tribal governments as democratically elected governments, rather than as corporations.

By the turn from the 20th to the 21st century, *sovereignty* and *nation* had again become key terms, not only for reformed Indigenous governments, but also for critical Indigenous scholars. As Lenape scholar Joanne Barker (2005) noted, "sovereignty" became a "particularly valued term" for Indigenous peoples. It was "a term around which analyses of indigenous histories and cultures were organized and whereby indigenous activists articulated their agendas for social change" (p. 18). It remains, however, a problematic term, as it necessitates "translating indigenous epistemologies about law, governance, and culture through the discursive rubric of sovereignty," which is, of course, a wholly Western term (p. 19). For this reason, Mohawk scholar Taiaiake Alfred (2005) argued that "sovereignty" is inappropriate as a political objective for indigenous peoples" (p. 38). According to Alfred, Indigenous peoples would be better served by focusing on "nationhood" as understood in their own Indigenous terms, rather than in terms set forth by Euro-American systems like Canada and the United States. "The challenge for indigenous peoples in building appropriate postcolonial governing systems is to disconnect the notion of sovereignty from its Western, legal roots and to transform it" (p. 42).

Building on Alfred's concept of Indigenous nationhood, Ojibwe rhetorician Scott Richard Lyons (2010) has suggested a conception of nationhood based on citizenship in an Indigenous community, as set forth by ethicist Herman Van Gunsteren (1988, p. 732). Citizenship in an Indigenously construed nation, Lyons contends, is constructed by answering two questions: "Who am I?" and "What should I do?" The answer to the first determines national identity. The answer to the second is determined by whatever a nation requires or expects of its citizens for the betterment of the nation, and consequently, the betterment of its citizens (pp. 172–173). This conception of nationhood, Lyons argues, leaves issues such as adherence to traditional cultures and practices, modernization, government, and citizenship requirements—all issues that have vexed modern Indigenous tribal collectives (pp. 73–109)—to the national citizens themselves, rather than to potentially foreign standards.

It is just such a standard for Indigenous nationhood as Lyons proposed that Barack Obama appears to recognize in his presidential rhetoric. I would suggest that, when candidate Obama called the Cherokee Freedmen controversy a sovereignty issue, he misspoke to some degree. Indigenous tribes still meet neither the Pindarian, Schmittian, nor Agambenian standards for sovereignty. But they are practicing nationhood, sometimes to such a degree that it offends Euro-American sensibilities. Such is the case with the Freedmen issue, wherein Cherokees' chosen identity conflicts with the modern American understanding of racial justice. Obama may not even have agreed with the Cherokees' exclusion of the Freedmen from the tribe. He may, in fact, have found it abhorrent. But he viewed it as a choice made by citizens, answering, in a very democratic manner, the questions of who they are, and what they should do. It was, in fact, an issue—not of Indigenous sovereignty—but of Indigenous nationhood. In the following section, I will examine Obama's presidential discourse vis-à-vis the Indigenous peoples in the United States. I will demonstrate that President Obama rhetorically constructs the United States as a nation-state consisting of a plurality of nations, all of whom contribute to a broader American ethos, yet still retain their Indigenous national identities.

Nations within the nation-state

On November 5, 2009, President Barack Obama hosted the first annual Tribal Nations Conference, the largest gathering of tribal leaders in the history of the United States. Hosting the conference was, itself, a significant exhibition of presidential rhetoric, a statement of recognition, even respect, for Indigenous communities as nations—communities with cultural and governmental practices uniquely their own. The gathering was a manifestation of Executive Order 13175, titled "Consultation and Coordination with Indian Tribal Governments," issued by President Bill Clinton in November of 2000, during his final months as president. The executive order had been ignored, however, by Clinton's successor, George W. Bush.

Bush, in fact, had experienced a less than amicable relationship with tribal nations during his 8 years in office. Speaking at the 2004 Unity: Journalists of Color convention in Washington, DC, Bush was asked by an Indigenous journalist what tribal sovereignty meant in the 21st century. The president's response was, "Tribal sovereignty means just that; it's sovereign. You're a—you've been given sovereignty, and you're viewed as a sovereign entity" (Kamb, 2004, para. 5). The response, undoubtedly not due to the slippage and casuistic stretching of the term *sovereignty* discussed earlier, did not sit well with Indigenous Americans. Jacqueline Johnson, executive director of the Washington, DC-based National Congress of American Indians, summed up the Indigenous response to the presidential gaffe when she pointed out that sovereignty was "not something that was given to us. As tribes, we see sovereignty as something we've always had" (Kamb, 2004, para. 8). Despite the aforementioned preference by many critical Indigenous scholars to speak of nationhood rather than sovereignty, Bush's response was a clear illustration to many

Indigenous Americans of an administration that was out of touch with Indigenous discourses and concerns.

In his opening remarks at the 2009 inaugural Tribal Nations Conference, President Obama passingly noted the inactivity of the Bush administration in the implementation of Executive Order 13175, thus drawing a clear distinction between the Bush presidency's Indigenous policy and his own. Noticeably missing from Obama's address was that slippery term, sovereignty, which he eschewed for the more cumbersome but realistic description of tribes as entities who are more empowered "when they make their own decisions." Multiple times, President Obama modified the language used in Clinton's executive order from "government-to-government" to "nation-to-nation," thus acknowledging the nationhood of Indigenous tribes while still presenting them as members of a broader American society:

> I'm absolutely committed to moving forward with you and forging a new and better future together. It's a commitment that's deeper than our unique nation-to-nation relationship. It's a commitment to getting this relationship right, so that you can be full partners in the American economy, and so your children and your grandchildren can have an equal shot at pursuing the American Dream.

This presentation of Indigenous tribes as nations within a nation demonstrates a particular genre of rhetoric, a calling-into-being of a people that Maurice Charland (1987) termed *constitutive rhetoric* (p. 134). Charland drew heavily from Michael McGee's (1975) contention that political collectives— "the people" adhering to a particular ideology—are "more process than phenomenon," and remain "so long as the rhetoric which defined them has force" (p. 242). Charland argued that such a collective does not, in fact, exist in nature, but "only within a discursively constituted history" that, at the same time, constitutes the collective's identity (p. 137).

In her examination of American identity construction in nineteenth century presidential rhetoric, Vanessa Beasley (2004) illustrated how the national constitutive rhetoric of presidents Grover Cleveland, William McKinley, and Theodore Roosevelt presented Indigenous Americans as a counter-example of the ideal American identity. In 19th century America, Indigenes possessed qualities such as collectivistic governance that were decidedly un-American, yet were still somehow a tangential aspect of Americanness (pp. 96–105). Beasley concludes that such "exclusivist inclusion" allows rhetors to disregard issues of inequality and national responsibility, and resort to a "we gave you a chance to join us" argument when such issues are broached (p. 105). Even the seemingly more humane policies of President Franklin Roosevelt's "New Deal for the Indian" were couched in terms of corporatism, imposing a model of American entrepreneurialism on ostensibly tribally operated governments (Nabakov, 1999, p. 305; Oklahoma Indian Welfare Act, 1936, p. 1967). Both Robert Berkhofer (1978) and Fergus Bordewich (1997) argued persuasively that Indigenous Americans have, throughout the history of the United States, served alternatively as models of particular kinds of American citizenship—especially for arguments espousing spirituality and environmentalism—and models of savage otherness. Be it Hollywood movies, sports mascots, or presidential oratory, Indigenous Americans have been stuck somewhere between Americanness and otherness—noble enough to be role models, but ignoble enough to be feared, eliminated, or at the very least, marginalized (Berkhofer, 1978, p. 60, p. 83).

In his address to the inaugural Tribal Nations Conference, however, President Obama celebrates a nations-within-a-nation concept that openly acknowledges the marginalization of Indigenous Americans, while recognizing that the United States, as the nation-state we know today, began with the nations of the "first Americans." He presents himself as a living example of the nations-within concept with a story of his "adoption" while campaigning in 2008 by Hartford and Mary Black Eagle, members of the Crow Nation. Although this adoption story may seem to emerge straight out of a mid-twentieth century Hollywood script, it does serve to create some common ground between President Obama and his Indigenous audience. It demonstrates that the nations-within concept is more than discourse—it is lived by people who can engage culturally, linguistically, and governmentally in their tribal nations while likewise engaging fully with American society and governance in all possible ways: "Only in America could the adoptive son of Crow Indians grow up to become President of the United States" (Obama, 2009). This lived binationality is further supported by the president's introduction of three recent presidential appointees: Native American Policy Advisor, Cherokee Nation member Kimberly Teehee; Deputy Assistant Secretary of Indian Affairs Jodi Gillette, a member of the Standing Rock Sioux Tribe; and Assistant Secretary for Indian Affairs, Pawnee Nation member Larry Echo Hawk. Moreover, each of the Tribal Nations Conferences hosted by President Obama included workshop sessions attended by tribal leaders and administrative leaders of all federal departments that deal with Indigenous issues. These sessions allowed—again, for the first time—face-to-face, nation-to-nation consultation between Indigenous leadership and federal leadership.

The positive response to President Obama's speech indicated by Indigenous leaders' comments during the question/answer session illustrates their appreciation for the president's understanding of tribes, not just as ethnic groups, but as nations, each with unique concerns. But, as much as the speech may demonstrate President Obama's respect for Indigenous Americans, it says a great deal more about his conception of the United States itself. To speak of nation-to-nation relationships with entities within the geographic borders of the United States is an unprecedented presidential reconstitution of American identity. It is a rhetorical move that militates against the sort of nationalism that can often operate with a double-edge. Such nationalism can inspire voluntary, participatory citizenship behaviors, while at the same time precipitating authoritarianism and intolerance (Li & Brewer, 2004, pp. 727–728; Van Evera, 1994). President Obama's nationalism is, instead, a nationalism with some tension. On one hand, it accepts the sovereignty of the United States, in the Pindarian sense. The United States is, without doubt, the world's most potentially violent nation. But on the other, it is a nationalism that concedes the temporal foundations of the United States to other nations and recognizes their continued existence. President Obama foregoes the ontological certainty of the monolithic *nation* and presents the term as a process-oriented epistemic methodology for addressing issues within "distinct, independent political communities," to harken back to John Marshall's 1832 definition. President Obama more clearly defined this process-oriented conception of nationhood in his address to the second Tribal Nations Conference in 2010: "What matters far more than words—what matters far more than any resolution or declaration—are actions to match those words. And that's what this conference is about … That's the standard I expect my administration to be held to" (Obama, 2010).

He continued by associating the multinational aspect of United Stats/Indigenous relations he had laid out the previous year with the motto of the United States itself. Nation-to-nation relationships between the United States and tribes are, the president said, "a matter of upholding an ideal that has always defined who we are as Americans. *E pluribus unum*. Out of many, one" (Obama, 2010). But, unlike previous presidents who saw the American "one" being augmented by Indigenes who had forsaken or been divested of their tribal customs, President Obama presented America as a nation that is co-constituted by Indigenes—not in spite of their Indigenous nationalities—but because of them. As he put it most clearly, 4 years later at the sixth Tribal Nations Conference: "Each [Indigenous nation] is a unique and cherished part of our American community. To all of my adopted Crow brothers and sisters—*hine wabeh itchik*. It is a good day" (Obama, 2014). For the attending tribal leaders whose nations had once served presidential rhetoric as examples of a most un-American collectivism, to be recognized as both constitutive elements of the United States and as independent nations must, indeed, have signified a good day.

In all seven of the Tribal Nations Conference addresses President Obama has made at the time of this writing, he has never wavered on two key points. First, he recognizes that the United States is the sovereign over all the territory within its borders. He concedes that, in the past, such sovereignty has been exercised irresponsibly and inhumanely against Indigenous tribes. But he never denies, or apologizes for, his position as the commander of the violence that insures that sovereignty. Second, he never equates that sovereignty with an exclusive United States nationhood. We are a nation-state, he acknowledges, the most expansive in the world. But we are made up of many nations—that is, many life-ways and traditions that have their own unique ways of viewing and dealing with the world around them. The fact that the newest and most populous of those nations happens to also be the most dominant does not, in President Obama's view, negate the concerns of the more than five-hundred others.

Were President Obama's inclusion of Indigenous nations in his rhetorically constituted America relegated to the annual Tribal Nations Conferences, it could easily be written off as political pandering. But his most visible recognition of Indigenous nationalism not only solidified his nations-within stance on American Indigeneity, it also raised the ire of Euro-Americans who espoused a more colonizing view of the United States.

In August of 2015, the White House Press Secretary's office announced that President Obama would, on the following day, officially rename Mt. McKinley, the tallest mountain in the United States. The mountain was named in 1896 to honor William McKinley, the 25th president of the United States. But previously, the mountain had been known by the Indigenous Koyukon Athabascan people as "Denali," or "the great one." Denali is not only a prominent feature of their landscape, it is also a key element of the Koyukon Athabascan's creation story (White House, 2015). Although elected representatives from the state of Alaska had been attempting to have the mountain renamed Denali since 1975, federal legislation to that effect had failed to pass. President Obama's executive order authorized the recognition of the mountain's precolonization Indigenous title, Denali. The order, however, struck some as an insult. Federal lawmakers from McKinley's home state of Ohio publicly expressed their disappointment, and front-running Republican candidate for the 2016 presidential election, Donald Trump, vowed to reverse the name change, should he be elected (LoBianco, 2015).

Certainly, the executive decision to indigenize the name of the highest point in the United States served as political grist for right-wing politicians vying for support in a heated lead-up to a presidential election year. But more importantly to the argument presented herein, the name change was an enactment of the very nations-within rhetoric President Obama had already been presenting at Tribal Nations Conferences since 2009. Titles, as rhetorical theorist Kenneth Burke noted (1969), call forth a desired response in an audience (p. 86). Be they applied to people, places, or things, titles indicate where priorities lie for both the presenters thereof, and for the audience of that presenter. The response to the change-of-title for the geographical high-point in the United States was likewise audience-dependent. To the Alaskan Indigenous audience, the name change served as vindication. It was a decolonizing strategy, albeit implemented by the leader of an historically colonizing government. It acknowledged the Indigenous presence on the Alaskan landscape long before English-speaking people arrived (Hetter, 2015). For political opponents of President Obama, the new title, Denali—a word that is decidedly not Euro-American in derivation—was yet one more example of questionably patriotic activities by the president. Barack Obama's own name is similarly not Euro-American, and his very right to occupy the presidency was questioned by some on the far right of the American political spectrum well into his first term of office (Baker, 2015; Levy, 2015). For some, the name change may have seemed like a non-issue. After all, Denali had been the name suggested to replace McKinley by Alaskan lawmakers both Democrat and Republican for over four decades. Moreover, the name had for many years been appropriated for a popular General Motors sport-utility vehicle and was not wholly unknown to the American public.

But as presidential rhetoric, as the locus of a presidential act that carried significant political ramifications, Denali spoke volumes. Certainly, its replacement of McKinley was an acknowledgement that the United States is, despite an historic narrative to the contrary, not a nation-state exclusively for the benefit and recognition of Euro-American peoples and practices. But it was also an acknowledgement that the Indigenous peoples of Alaska are American people, not foreign others—even if their names for mountains may sound a bit exotic to Western ears. The Koyukon Athabascan people matter. Their places matter. Their beliefs matter, and their titles matter. Their rhetoric matters. An official adoption by the United States government of their name for the most prominent mountain in America is not, as President Obama's political opponents argued, unpatriotic (Levy, 2015). It is most patriotic because the Koyukon Athabascans are, as the president has proposed in his Tribal Nations Conference speeches, most assuredly Americans. In effect, President Obama's adoption of Denali reifies his constitutive rhetoric vis-à-vis Indigenous Americans. It animates—not just in Indigenous America, but for all Americans—the contributions of Indigenous peoples to the United States. More importantly, however, it animates the American-ness of Indigenes living within the American nation-state.

By the end of 2015, the penultimate year of his presidency, Barack Obama had visited more Indigenous nation communities than any other sitting president. At the Tribal Nations Conference that year, he once again presented his nations-within conception of United States/Indigenous relations. Again contrasting this stance with those of presidents-past, he noted that,

> I've said that while we couldn't change the past, working together, nation-to-nation, we could build a better future. I believed this not only because America has a moral obligation to do right by the tribes and treaty obligations, but because the success of our tribal communities is tied up with the success of America as a whole. (Obama, 2015)

President Obama concluded his 2015 address by referencing a longstanding controversy in the American public sphere—Indigenous mascots of sports teams. Indigenous leaders, scholars, and citizens have long decried the name "Redskins" as the moniker for Washington D.C.'s professional football team. The president had said in 2013 that team owners should "think about changing" the name. Despite claims by the team's owner that the term is an expression of respect, many Indigenous Americans see it as a slur that refers back to a time when bounties were paid by colonial governments for the skins of dead Indigenes (Martinez, 2013). In his Tribal Nations Conference address, however, President Obama clarified his opposition to offensive sports mascots. As the 2015 conference was dedicated to issues of Indigenous youth and education, the president asserted that changing offensive sports team names was a debt owed to young tribal members, not only because they are Indigenous, but because they are Americans who deserve to have both of their national identities valued: "[T]hat's really what this Tribal Nations Conference is about—extraordinary young people representing the promise not just of their tribes or of Indian Country, but of the United States—because ultimately, we're one family and these kids are our kids" (Obama, 2015).

President Obama's implementation of the Tribal Nations Conference is unprecedented in American presidential history. But his rhetorical inclusion, his constitutive-ness of Indigeneity in American culture, may be one of his most enduring legacies. Certainly, he has spent more time in "Indian Country"—still an official federal designation despite its waning use in American parlance. His administration, through the conferences, has consulted more productively with tribal leaders on issues of concern to tribal governments. But the most striking contrast of his Indigenous policy with that of previous administrations has been his recognition of "nation," not as a term of division, but of inclusion.

Conclusion

"Think about it for a second," Swinomish Nation Chairman Brian Cladoosby urged the audience at the 2012 Tribal Nations Conference, where he was introducing President Barack Obama. "The president loves basketball. He has an Indian name "One Who Helps People Throughout the Land,' given to him by the aforementioned "adopted" Crow Nation family (Zeleney, 2008)], he knows what it's like to be poor and he hasn't forgotten where he came from. And his theme song is 'Hail to the Chief.' I think he definitely qualifies as the first American Indian president" (Sink, 2012).

Of course, Cladoosby was having a bit of good-natured fun with his introductory comments, but there is substantial data to indicate that Barack Obama may well be the most Indigenous-friendly president the nations have ever known. Every agency in the Obama administration has developed detailed plans and procedures for consulting with Indigenous nations prior to any government action that may affect those nations. These new agency policies are authorized by the same act—Executive Order 13175, originally signed by President Bill Clinton (2000)—that facilitated the Tribal Nations Conferences. Such policies manifest President Obama's nations-within rhetoric in tangible ways. The Obama administration's Affordable Care Act, perhaps the most publicized law passed during his eight-year administration, includes a lesser-known provision, the Indian Healthcare Improvement Act, which facilitates care to Indigenous communities. Both the Department of Commerce and the Department of Agriculture have implemented programs dedicated to bringing high-speed broadband internet service to Indigenous communities. Law enforcement agencies have introduced programs aimed at reducing the occurrence of domestic violence in tribal areas. Businesses owned by American Indigenes received nearly $8.7 billion-worth of federal contracts. The Small Business Administration loaned nearly $328 million to Indigenously owned companies. Seven Indigenous Americans were named to administrative posts in the Obama presidency. Several longstanding Indigenous legal claims against the United States were settled during President Obama's terms. The first, *Keepseagle v. Vilsack*, provided $760 million to Indigenous American farmers and ranchers who have been discriminated against by the Department of Agriculture in past decades. Second, *Cobell v. Salazar*, a class action lawsuit over insufficient federal management of land held in trust for tribal nations, will provide $3.4 billion to tribes, with $1.4 billion going to the plaintiffs and two billion dollars going toward the repurchase of land distributed out of tribal ownership under the early twentieth century allotment process. That land will, for the first time in over a century, be held communally by tribes. Finally, the U.S. government agreed to pay the Osage Nation $380 million to compensate the tribe for federal mismanagement of resources (White House, n.d.).

Could more have been done? According to James Anaya, special reporter for the United Nations on Indigenous rights, yes. In 2012, he recommended a return of land to Indigenous tribes in the United States. The dispossession of tribal land over centuries has, Anaya noted, led to a breakdown of traditional Indigenous societies that has, in a cyclical nature, led to stereotypes that perpetuate systemic racism against Indigenous Americans:

> The idea that is often projected through the mainstream media and among public figures that indigenous peoples are either gone or as a group are insignificant or that they're out to get benefits in terms of handouts, or their communities and cultures are reduced to casinos, which are just flatly wrong. (McGreal, 2012)

This systemic racial discrimination is perhaps the most pernicious effect of the unfettered exercise of American sovereignty in the eighteenth and nineteenth centuries. It could be assuaged and restoration of Indigenous lifeways begun, Anaya contends, with the return of tribal lands. A wholesale land return is not likely to occur any time in the foreseeable future, as no members of Congress had agreed to meet with Anaya as part of his investigation. He did remark that the Obama administration had exhibited "exemplary cooperation," but that there were still "deeper issues that need to be addressed" beyond the meager land returns that were part of the abovementioned legal settlements (McGreal, 2012).

As President Obama has acknowledged at every Tribal Nations Conference, the injustices perpetrated by the United States against Indigenous peoples will be a long time in resolving. But a promising beginning of that resolution is the marked change in presidential rhetoric concerning Indigenous Americans. As I have argued here, President Obama has presented Indigenous peoples as nations within the nation-state of the United States, as constitutive members of American society. In doing so, he has presented the United States as a "state of nations," a collective of unique community/nations, rather than a monolithic sovereign. It is a unique presidential rhetorical treatment of Indigenous Americans in the twenty-first century. It is a stark contrast to the presentation of Indigenes by nineteenth and twentieth century presidents, who used tribal peoples as examples of decidedly un-American existences (Beasley, 2004, pp. 96–105). From his address to the inaugural Tribal Nations Conference in 2009 to his renaming of the United States' tallest mountain, President Obama has recognized, and responded to, the exigencies of the Indigenous constitutive nations of the United States. Time, and subsequent presidential administrations, will tell if the nations-within concept is maintained. Should it be, history will no doubt situate the beginnings of that concept in the presidency of Barack Obama.

References

Agamben, G. (1998). *Homo sacer: Sovereign power and bare life* (Heller-Roazen, D. Trans.). Stanford, CA: Stanford University Press.

Alfred, T. (2005). In J. Barker (Ed.) *Sovereignty matters: Locations of contestation and possibility in Indigenous struggles for self-determination* (pp. 32–50). Lincoln, NE: University of Nebraska Press.

Baker, P. (2015, July 22). Kenya trip takes Obama back to a complex part of himself. *The New York Times*. Retrieved from http://www.nytimes.com/2015/07/23/world/africa/africa-trip-takes-obama-back-to-a-complex-part-of-himself.html?ref=topics&_r=1

Barker, J. (2005). For whom sovereignty matters. In J. Barker (Ed.) *Sovereignty matters: Locations of contestation and possibility in Indigenous struggles for self-determination* (pp. 1–31). Lincoln, NE: University of Nebraska Press.

Beasley, V. B. (2004). *You, the people: American national identity in presidential rhetoric*. College Station, TX: Texas A&M University Press.

Berkhofer, R. F. (1978). *The white man's Indian*. New York, NY: Vintage.

Bordewich, F. (1997). *Killing the white man's Indian: Reinventing native Americans at the end of the twentieth century*. New York, NY: Anchor.

Burke, K. (1969). *A rhetoric of motives*. Berkeley, CA: University of California Press.

Charland, M. (1987). Constitutive rhetoric: The case of the *Peuple Québécois. Quarterly. Journal of Speech, 73*, 133–150.

Cherokee Nation v. Georgia, 30 U.S. (5 Pet.) 1 (1831).

Clinton, W. J. (2000, November 6). Executive order 13175 consultation and coordination with Indian tribal governments. Retrieved from https://www.gpo.gov/fdsys/pkg/FR-2000-1109/pdf/00-29003.pdf

Cobell v. Salazar, D. C. Cir. 11-5202 (2012).

Deloria, V. (1969). *Custer died for your sins*. Norman, OK: University of Oklahoma Press.

Hetter, K. (2015, September 4). Beyond Denali: Restoring native American names. *CNN*. Retrieved from http://www.cnn.com/2015/09/04/travel/denali-renaming-natural-sites-feat/

Kamb, L. (2004, August 12). Bush's comment on tribal sovereignty creates a buzz. *Seattle PostIntelligencer*. Retrieved from http://www.seattlepi.com/local/article/Bush-s-comment-ontribal-sovereignty-creates-a-1151615.php

Keepseagle v. Vilsack, D. C. Cir. 14-5223 (2016).

Lake, R. (1983). Enacting red power: The consummatory function in Native American protestrhetoric. *Quarterly Journal of Speech, 69*, 127–142.

Levy, G. (2015, August 31). Obama's Denali name change infuriates Ohio lawmakers. *U.S. News & World Report*. Retrieved from http://www.usnews.com/news/articles/2015/08/31/hailing-mckinley-ohio-lawmakers-blast-obamas-denali-name-change

Li, Q., & Brewer, M. B. (2004). What Does It Mean to Be an American? Patriotism, nationalism, and American Identity after 9/11. *Political Psychology, 25*, 727–739.

LoBianco, T. (2015, August 31). Trump vows to reverse Obama's Mt. McKinley name change. *CNN*. Retreived from http://www.cnn.com/2015/08/31/politics/denali-mt-mckinley-reaction-renaming/

Lyons, S. R. (2010). *X-marks: Native signatures of assent*. Minneapolis, MN: University of MinnesotaPress.

McGee, M. C. (1975). In search of "the people": A rhetorical alternative. *Quarterly Journal ofSpeech, 61*, 235–249.

McGreal, C. (2012, May 4). US should return stolen land to Indian tribes, says United Nations. *The Guardian*. Retrieved from http://www.theguardian.com/world/2012/may/04/us-stolen-land-indian-tribes-un

Martinez, M. (2013, October 12). A slur or term of "honor"? Controversy heightens about Washington Redskins. *CNN*. Retrieved from http://www.cnn.com/2013/10/12/us/redskins-controversy/

Nabakov, P. (1999). *Native American testimony: A chronicle of Indian-White relations fromprophesy to the present, 1492–2000* (3rd ed.). New York, NY: Penguin.

Obama, B. H. (2009, November 5). *Opening address at Tribal Nations Conference*. Washington, DC.

Obama, B. H. (2010, December 16). *Opening address at Tribal Nations Conference*. Washington, DC.

Obama, B. H. (2014, December 3). *Opening address at Tribal Nations Conference*. Washington, DC.

Obama, B. H. (2015, November 5). *Opening address at Tribal Nations Conference*. Washington, DC.

Oklahoma Indian Welfare Act. United States Cong. 74 Cong. (1936) (enacted).

Schmitt, C. (1974). *Das nomos von der erde* [The nomos of the earth]. Berlin, Germany: Duncker & Humbolt.

Sink, J. (2012, December 5). Tribal leader calls Obama "first American Indian president." *The Hill*. Retrieved from http://thehill.com/blogs/blog-briefing-room/news/271273swinomish-nation-chairman-introduces-obama-as-first-american-indian-president

Sturm, C. (2002). *Blood politics: Race, culture, and identity in the Cherokee Nation of Oklahoma*. Berkeley, CA: University of California Press.

Tishkov, V. (2000). Forget the "nation": Post-nationalist understanding of nationalism. *Ethnic and Racial Studies, 23*, 625–650.

van Evera, S. (1994). Hypotheses on nationalism and war. *International Security, 18*(4), 5–39.

Van Gunsteren, H. R. (1988, July). Admission to citizenship. *Ethics, 98*(4), 731–741.

Watson, D. (2008). Sen. Barack Obama and the Cherokee Freedmen: Politics as usual. *The Hill*. Retrieved from http://thehill.com/opinion/op-ed/7717-senbarack-obama-andthe-cherokee-freedmen-politics-as-usual

White House. (2015, August 30). *President will announce renaming of Mt. McKinley to Denali* [Press release]. Washington, DC: Author.

White House. (n.d.). *Obama administration record for American Indians and Alaskan natives*. Retrieved from https://www.whitehouse.gov/sites/default/files/docs/american_indians_and_alaska_nativs_community_record_0.pdf

Worcester v. Georgia. 31 U.S. 515 (1832).

Zeleney, J. (2008, May 19). Obama adopted by native Americans. *The New York Times*. Retrieved from http://thecaucus.blogs.nytimes.com/2008/05/19/obama-adopted-by-native-americans/?_r=0

Michelle Obama: Exploring the Narrative

Marian Meyers and Carmen Goman

ABSTRACT

When Michelle Obama was first introduced to the American public in 2008, she was depicted in the media as an unpatriotic, stereotypical, angry Black woman. Today, she is more popular than the president. This study examines the narrative about Michelle Obama created by the first lady and the White House through YouTube videos uploaded in an attempt to redefine her in ways that are more acceptable to the public. The authors examine that narrative in videos posted by the White House, mainstream news and entertainment outlets, and allied organizations, with a focus on the intersectionality of gender, race and class in her story. The findings indicate that Obama's story reflects a neoliberal narrative framed by two themes: (a) the American Dream is achievable through education, hard work, and perseverance; and (b) motherhood and family are primary. Within this neoliberal narrative, racism and poverty are obstacles to be overcome through making the right choices, and gender is viewed through the narrow lens of motherhood rather than gendered inequalities. This narrative is both shaped and constrained by Obama's race, class background, and gender, as well as the goal of creating a more acceptable public persona.

The U.S. public's introduction to Michelle Obama occurred during the 2008 election campaign, when her husband, Barack Obama, was running for president. She became, as *TIME Magazine* reported, "a favorite target of conservatives, who attack her with an exuberance that suggests there are no taboos anymore" (Gibbs & Newton-Small, 2008). Jamil Smith (2015) noted in *The New Republic* that the media, faced with the prospect of a Black first lady, "almost immediately ran rife with racial insults—blatant, coded, and along all points in between—a flow of invective that has never really ceased" (p. 10). She was said to be unpatriotic and was accused by right-wing radio personality Rush Limbaugh of referring to White people as "Whitey" (Pickler, 2008, p. A2). Fox News called her "Obama's baby mama," in addition to accusing her of giving her husband a "terrorist fist jab" when they bumped knuckles at a campaign rally (Pickler, 2008, p. A2). The conservative *National Review* magazine called her "Mrs. Grievance" and claimed she stoked discontent (Steyn, 2008).

And in a satire of the ways she had been stereotyped as an angry, militant, unpatriotic and disgruntled Black woman, a cover illustration in *The New Yorker* magazine depicted her wearing combat fatigues, a gun and ammunition belt slung over her shoulder, her hair in a large Afro, and a painting of Osama bin Laden over a fireplace in which the U.S. flag was burning. She and her husband, he dressed in a turban and robe, were bumping fists.

These depictions and the negative public perceptions of the potential first lady during the 2008 presidential campaign "so stirred up the Obama campaign's PR machine that the future first lady had to be re-choreographed into a more palatable routine; in short, she appears to have been 'handled,' 'softened' in tone and image" (Spillers, 2009, p. 308). Michelle Obama's outspokenness during the 2008 campaign had been controversial (Shoop, 2010), and a new, more acceptable narrative of who she was had to be created. This involved granting numerous interviews to traditional media, and the Obama campaign—"renowned for its sophisticated use of the Internet and YouTube" (Strangelove, 2010, p. 139)—also deftly deployed YouTube videos to bring its message and her story straight to the public. Mortensen (2015) pointed out that, "While journalists are losing gatekeeping control, others—in this case, the White House—are gaining control in influencing audiences perceptions" of the first lady by uploading visuals to the internet. Obama[1] gained an additional online presence in 2012 when she provided parenting advice on the women's website iVillage (Clark, 2012).

The success of efforts to change Michelle Obama's narrative are reflected in the polls, with the first lady becoming more popular than the president. For example, 2014 polls show the president's approval rating at 48% to first lady's 66% (Brown, 2014). The fact that Michelle Obama and her staff were able to change her image attests to their skill, effectiveness, and agility in deploying the internet.

And yet, the invective, as Smith (2015) pointed out, has not stopped. For example, in 2011, Limbaugh claimed that the first lady and her family had displayed "a little bit of uppity-ism," a term, Smith noted, "used to describe a black person who doesn't know her or his 'place'" (p. 10). Given such ongoing attacks on the first lady, it is no surprise that the White House continued its online efforts to tell the story of Michelle Obama.

This study examines that narrative of the U.S.'s first African American first lady as constructed in YouTube video clips. It asks how Obama and the White House[2] sought to portray the story of the first lady, as well as how mainstream media outlets and allied organizations—that is, those institutions and groups before whom Obama appeared as a keynote speaker or panelist—contributed to this narrative. In addition, it views this narrative from an intersectional perspective that sees race, gender, class, and other aspects of identity as interconnected.

Although previous studies have examined the representation and roles of Michelle Obama online (e.g., see Meyers, 2013; Mortensen, 2015), none have explored the narrative or the major themes within the story the White House and Michelle Obama herself have told about who she is. And although those studies concluded that the White House framed the first lady within the context of domesticity, this study argues that Obama's use of anecdotes about her family and personal struggles reflects a neoliberal ideology that advocates for individual responsibility and initiative. As such, it goes beyond roles and stereotypes to explore the underlying meaning and ideology within the narrative. The findings also reveal two primary themes within the first lady's story: education, hard work, and perseverance are necessary for success; and motherhood and family are primary. In addition, by applying an intersectional perspective, it is possible to see the role of race, gender, and class within Obama's neoliberal narrative. Racism and poverty are seen as obstacles to be overcome, but they are not insurmountable if the individual makes the right choices. Gender inequities are viewed through the lens of motherhood and the need to balance family and career, rather than within a broader, gendered context that addresses sexual harassment, violence, and discrimination. Obama's narrative is no doubt constrained by the imperative to make her more palatable to a public inclined to see her as a stereotypical, angry Black woman. As such, this study has much to say about how society views Black women, the limitations they face, and the political work of shaping public narratives.

Literature review

Michelle Obama's two signature initiatives as first lady are her Let's Move campaign to combat childhood obesity, and Joining Forces, a program that assists military families and veterans. Cherlin (2014) pointed out that, in the fall of 2010, Obama wanted to do more and so directed her staff to review her options and to hire "a top-flight communications director" to lead the effort. Cherlin said this decision was driven by the fact that "some palace watchers had been underwhelmed so far by her agenda, and this was an opportunity to prove these critics wrong." He also stated that in choosing public events, Obama is extremely cautious, particularly concerning "her family public life," and requires that all events have a "concrete, achievable goal" and "guarantee results." Details and every move are planned months in advance, with speeches finalized weeks ahead of time:

> Mrs. Obama depends on structure to support her public warmth—the ease with which she'll pick up a hula-hoop, say, or do the Dougie with school kids. That mandate to be deliberate in all things has been enshrined into East Wing operating procedure ... Staff knew that every event should produce positive coverage, and that all angles had to be exhaustively researched and gamed out (not easy with a team of less than 30). (Cherlin, 2014)

Parry-Giles and Parry-Giles (1999) referred to the "art and practice of political image construction" as meta-imaging, a form of political discourse in which "campaign outsiders attempt to get 'inside' presidential campaigns to unmask the image and the 'real' candidate" (p. 29). This occurs through campaigns granting journalists exclusive interviews and behind-the-scenes access to candidates or other insiders who can shed light on the "real" person behind the image. The results, the authors pointed out, "appear as good investigative journalism or diligent documentary filmmaking," but are in reality "highly managed and controlled by the campaigns to put the best image forward of a candidate and a campaign" (p. 29)—or, in this case, the president's wife.

Despite the administration's efforts to shape Obama's meta-image, scholars who have examined Obama's representation in the media generally have concluded that it continues to draw on racist and sexist stereotypes of Black women. For example, Lugo-Lugo and Bloodsworth-Lugo (2011) stated that Obama "has been uniquely positioned at the intersection between enduring perceptions of Black women within the United States and new, post-9/11 constructions of threat/danger to country and its citizenry—rendering her 'unsafe'" (p. 203). They add that she appears as a threat in two ways: (a) her "preoccupation with her daughters rather than with the campaign or the country" rejects the Mammy stereotype of the self-sacrificing Black woman who puts the needs of White people above her own and her family (p. 210); and (b) she embodies the "threatening/unsafe stereotype of the Jezebel" by virtue of her physically attractive and toned body (pp. 213–214).

For Harris-Perry (2011), Obama is "the most visible contemporary example of an African American woman working to stand straight" in a room warped by racism and sexism (p. 271), a room that "attempts to frame her within the common trope of hypersexuality," as when Fox News called her "Barack's baby mama," or as a stereotypical "angry black woman" (pp. 274–275). Harris-Perry further explained that these frames draw on myths about Black women in ways that have shaped public perceptions of Obama's body, motherhood, and marriage:

> In each case, she made a number of choices to deflect, resist, redirect, or accommodate these anxieties about her black womanhood. Because her efforts were so public, they provide insight into the efforts of one African American woman to stand straight in a crooked room. They also suggest the limitations of individual strategies to challenge deeply embedded myths. (p. 277)

The limitations imposed on Obama are a reflection of the fact that, as the first African American first lady, she "is constrained by different stereotypes from those that inhibit white women" (Harris-Perry, 2011, p. 289). And although Obama has been "highly visible" in crafting "a more traditional role for herself" that involves "relatively safe issues like childhood literacy, ending childhood obesity, advocacy for women and girls, and support for military families" (p. 289), the first lady's dedication to and focus on her children are acts of resistance that challenge the Mammy stereotype.

In addition, in studies of Obama's portrayal online, Mortensen (2015) found that the White House portrayed her "in a more traditional light" than journalists (p. 62), and Meyers's (2013) examination of Obama's representation and roles in a wide range of YouTube clips from 2012 similarly found that White House-produced videos focused on domestic roles, presenting her as a committed mother, supportive wife, gracious hostess, and advocate for women and children. That study also identified a new stereotype within some videos about Obama uploaded primarily by right-wing, White males: the Powerful Black Bitch who "is dangerous, evil and in need of containment" (p. 68). The Powerful Black Bitch, according to Meyers

(2013), "has free reign to exercise her power to serve her own selfish interests, and she is able to extend her control beyond the black community to affect the lives of White people" (p. 68). However, that study, in focusing on roles and stereotypes, did not examine the narrative produced by the White House and Michelle Obama of who she is—a narrative shaped by Obama's race, class, and gender—nor did it explore themes or the underlying meaning within that narrative, as this study does.

Black feminist thought and intersectionality

The concept of intersectionality, derived from critical race and Black feminist theories, addresses the interaction of multiple categories of identity as sites of intersecting oppressions and privileges. As Gopaldas (2013) stated, intersectionality implies "that every person in society is positioned at the intersection of multiple identity structures and is thus subject to multiple social advantages and disadvantages" (p. 91). Black feminist scholars such as Patricia Hill Collins, bell hooks, and Angela Davis have long noted that racism and sexism cannot be understood as separate systems of oppression (see, e.g., Collins, 2005; Davis, 1998; hooks, 1981). As Crenshaw (1991) stated,

> An intersectional analysis argues that racial and sexual subordination are mutually reinforcing, that black women are commonly marginalized by a politics of race alone or a politics of gender alone, and that a political response to each form of subordination must at the same time be a political response to both. (p. 1283)

The intersectionality paradigm more recently has been expanded to include socially constructed identity categories beyond gender, race, and class, including nationality, sexuality, and dis/ability.[3] This understanding of intersectionality and the social construction of identity underscores the role of popular culture and the media, in particular, in fostering images and stereotypes that serve the interests of a White, ruling elite. These representations shift over time to reflect cultural and societal changes, with traditional stereotypes of Black women—such as the mammy who is devoted to her White family, the emasculating matriarch, the welfare mother, and the hypersexual Jezebel—continually updated to remain relevant (Collins, 2005).

Methodology

This study examined how the White House and Obama represented who she is to the public through YouTube video clips—the story they told about her life, how they told it, and the role gender, race, and class play in that narrative. YouTube video posted by the White House, allied organizations, and mainstream news and entertainment programs were included in this study. Media corporations exist in a symbiotic relationship with the White House in that they depend on the administration to provide news and programming to fill a seemingly insatiable 24-hour news and entertainment cycle. At the same time, the administration relies on the media to get its messages to the public. White House-produced clips not only serve as virtual "video press releases" in their own right, but they have a better chance of gaining news coverage than traditional campaign material (Palser, 2006, p. 84). Thus, it is important to examine YouTube clips from media organizations, as well as from the White House and allied organizations that featured talks and other appearances by Obama, to fully understand the narrative created by the White House and first lady.

The sampling method, similar to that used by Meyers (2013), involved downloading and saving to a file the first 100 YouTube clips retrieved on September 1, 2015, using "Michelle Obama" as the search term. After eliminating clips with duplicate footage and those not usable because they were not in English or did not contain any connection to the first lady, 62 video clips remained and were transcribed. An additional 23 were then eliminated because they did not meet the criteria for inclusion—that is, they were not posted by the White House, mainstream news organizations and televised entertainment programs, or allied organizations. In the end, 39 videos were examined using a combination of narrative analysis and the constant comparative method.

Narrative analysis is concerned not with why a story is being told, but how it is told through both form and content (Riessman, 1993, p. 2). "The challenge" in analyzing narrative, Riessman (1993) explained, "is to identify similarities across the moments into an aggregate, a summation" (p. 13). She emphasizes that "Any finding—a depiction of a culture, psychological process or social structure—exists in historical time, between subjects in relations of power" (p. 15). Reeves and Campbell (1994) also pointed out that contemporary narrative theory distinguishes between "story" and "discourse"—with story "concerned with 'what happens to whom'" and discourse asking "'how the story is told'" (p. 50). In analyzing journalistic narratives, Leitch (1986) stated, both form and content are important. The study of content can reveal which facts were omitted, and the study of form can help the analyst interpret the journalist's intent (Leitch, 1986). Form is revealed in the structure of the plot, the sequencing of events, the coherence and complexity of a narrative, and the choice of metaphors or language, none of which may be apparent in an analysis of the content (Lieblich, Tuval-Mashiach, & Zilber, 1998).

Four approaches to narrative analysis were identified by Lieblich and colleagues (1998): (a) a holistic-content reading, which looks at the meanings provided by the whole narrative, focusing on the one or two particular themes that emerge from throughout the narrative, or focusing on specific sections of the text within the context of the entire narrative; (b) a holistic-form reading, which focuses on how the plot is structured, how the story is developed, how it ascends or descends toward a specific event; (c) a categorical-content reading, also known as content analysis, which defines specific categories within the narrative and organizes sections into those categories; and (d) a categorical-form reading, which focuses on stylistic or linguistic characteristics of specific parts of the narrative.

This study uses a holistic-content reading that focuses on the whole narrative and the major themes that emerge within that narrative across the 39 YouTube clips examined. This is done, as Riessman (1993) explained, by identifying similarities or patterns "across the moments into an aggregate, a summation" (p. 13)—in this case, with an emphasis on the ways that gender, race, and class are reflected within the narrative. The constant comparative method (Glaser & Strauss, 1967) was used to ascertain this narrative's primary themes. In this method, also referred to as the grounded theory approach, themes and patterns emerge through the continuing comparison of videos until preliminary categories are eliminated and ultimately replaced with final categories as newer themes and patterns are derived from the comparison of texts.

Constructing the narrative

The mainstream news and entertainment media frequently covered the first lady's activities or interviewed her, while the White House and allied organizations uploaded YouTube clips of her speeches, panel discussions and other events that provided the opportunity for her to present her story directly to the public. She spoke at high school and college graduation ceremonies, and she appeared on televised talk shows, staged events at the White House, and even the popular children's TV show, *Sesame Street*, where she encouraged Grover, the furry blue monster, to eat a healthy breakfast. These appearances are highly scripted. Lynn Sweet, the Washington bureau chief of the *Chicago Sun Times*, stated in one of the videos: "Mrs. Obama is very disciplined. She rarely goes off script; she rarely puts herself in a position where she can have something happen unexpected" (CNN, 2013). Occasionally, Obama's appearances are repackaged on news programs and uploaded to YouTube by news organizations such as CNN or ABC News.

Analyzing Obama's narrative in YouTube clips revealed two primary themes: (a) the American Dream is achievable through education, hard work and perseverance; and (b) motherhood and family are primary. Each of these themes appeared dominant within different venues and before specific audiences. For example, in speaking to students, the theme of obtaining the American Dream was dominant, although her talks also could contain both themes. In addition, the same theme could emerge across different formats. For example, the importance of Obama's children to her would be mentioned in both a speech to students and a talk show appearance.

The narrative that emerges is an adaptation of neoliberal discourse, of "pulling yourself up by your own bootstraps" to overcome the obstacles of racism and poverty to achieve your goals. This narrative argues that hard work and resolve will inevitably lead to a successful, happy life, both professionally and personally—in the case of Michelle Obama, it led to her success as a lawyer, wife, and mother. Although neoliberal discourse generally assumes a level playing field, Obama's story recognizes the realities of multiple forms of discrimination while simultaneously acknowledging that support, luck, and faith also are prerequisites to achievement. The following sections draw on exemplars to illustrate the two major themes in this narrative.

Education, hard work, perseverance and the American Dream

Whether as the keynote speaker at commencement ceremonies, leading a panel discussion before a group of students or engaging in one-on-one discussion with a teenager in the White House, Obama emphasized her own background growing up on Chicago's South Side in a working-class family that had limited financial resources but was nonetheless committed to furthering her education, often despite the doubts and lack of support from school counselors and teachers. Working hard to further one's education as a means to achieve one's goals was consistent in Obama's talks to high school and college students, who she encouraged to stay focused and not be deterred by obstacles presented by poverty, racial discrimination, or personal circumstance. These talks were part of Obama's Reach Higher initiative[4] to encourage students to complete their education beyond high school by attending a professional training program, a community college or a 4-year college or university.

In video clips of commencement speeches at two high schools with racially diverse and economically disadvantaged student populations,[5] Obama recounted the challenges she overcame through hard work and determination which, she emphasized, led to an undergraduate degree from Princeton University and a law degree from Harvard. And she emphasized that they, too, can overcome any obstacles to achieve their goals if they work hard enough and have faith in themselves. For example, speaking to the Class of 2020 at the Columbia Heights Educational Campus in Washington, DC, the first lady urged students to commit to their education, fulfill their potential, and "unlock opportunities that you can't even begin to imagine" (The Book Archive, 2013). Her parents, she explained, never went to college and "didn't have a lot of money." But, she added,

> They encouraged me to enroll in one the best schools in Chicago. It was a school a lot like this one … my school was way across the other side of the city from where I lived. So at 6 a.m. every morning, I had to get on a city bus and ride for an hour, sometimes more, just to get to school. And I was willing to do that because I was willing to do whatever it took for me to go to college. I set my sights high. I decided I was going to Princeton but I quickly realized that for me, a kid like me, getting into Princeton wasn't just gonna happen on its own. (The Book Archive, 2013)

Instead, Obama emphasized, it took hard work, focus, determination and perseverance in the face of discouragement. When teachers "straight up told me that I was setting my sights too high" and that " I was never going to get into a school like Princeton," she added, it made her more determined: "When I encountered doubters, when people told me that I wasn't going to cut it, I didn't let that stop me. In fact, I did the opposite. I used that negativity to fuel me, to keep me going … And I am here today because I want you to know that my story can be your story" (The Book Archive, 2013).

A corollary to the theme of hard work and education as the route to success is that assistance from others, as well as luck and faith in one's self and God, are necessary. In a number of YouTube clips, she pointed out that she did not succeed on her own but had help from supportive parents, girlfriends, teachers, and others. In a video of the Beating the Odds summit at the White House, Obama credited her parents, in particular, with encouraging her education, stating that she was "blessed to have parents" who "knew that an investment in education was the best gift they could give me" (The White House, 2015).

In another YouTube clip, Obama discussed the challenges of being a first-generation college student. A belief in herself, despite naysayers and her own doubts, was essential—and she urged her listeners to believe in themselves. At Princeton, she worried that "maybe I just wasn't as smart" as classmates who came from affluent families and private schools (AussieNews1, 2014). But she soon realized:

> [this] was all in my head—I had just as much to contribute. I just had to have the confidence to believe in myself and the determination to work hard and ask for help when I needed it. So that's my message to all of you. No matter where you come from or how much money your family has, I want you to know that you can succeed in college and get your degree and then go on to build an incredible life for yourself. That's been my life story, and my husband's as well. And if you're willing to put in the time and the effort, I want you to know that it can be your story, too. (AussieNews1, 2014)

As part of her motivational "if I can do it, so can you" message to students, Obama routinely argues against the notion that she or her family are exceptional, stating that there are "millions of kids just like me, who don't get that encouragement, but have the same skills and ability" (AussieNews1, 2014). The difference between Obama and those who don't make it, she explains, is the support and encouragement they receive, as well as luck. Speaking at the Beating the Odds summit, Obama urged students not to be afraid to ask for assistance. She needed help, she explained, to navigate college and as first lady: "I cannot be first lady alone. I have a team of people. I have my mother living here. It's like—it's some days, I'm just like, 'Ma! Help me! Help me!'" (The White House, 2015). In an iVillage interview, Obama also stated that the support of family and friends has been essential throughout her life (iVillage, 2012). Her mother, she added, is "probably one of my closest advisers," as well as her friend, and friends from various stages of her life were her "saviors" because she could count on them when she was a working mother—and still does: "I just realized having some sort of support around, whether it was my mom or a set of friends, was essential to keeping me whole and not so angry or frustrated ... because you just share the load" (iVillage, 2012).

The idea that support is essential was echoed in a number of her speeches, including one to civic and business leaders in Chicago at a conference to address youth violence in that city. She told those gathered that the only "difference between growing up and becoming a lawyer, a mother, and first lady of the United States, and being shot dead at the age of 15" was that she had "a few more advantages" in the form of adults who "pushed" her, schools that prepared her, activities that engaged her, a community that supported her, and a neighborhood where she felt safe: "I started out with exactly the same aptitude—exactly the same intellectual, emotional capabilities—as so many of my peers" (The White House, 2013). In the end, she added, the support she received made all the difference.

Underlying the theme of education, hard work and perseverance as the route to the American Dream is the belief that the obstacles presented by racism and poverty can be overcome. In a speech to the predominantly Black graduating class of King College Preparatory High School on Chicago's South Side, where Obama was "born and raised," she exhorted students to use the scars they've suffered—the losses, sadness, and grief—to motivate them, as "folks in this community have always done" (McIntee, 2015).

Obama was most explicit about the impact of racism in a speech to the graduating class of Tuskegee University, a historically Black college. Here, she recounted the past humiliations and struggles endured by students and administrators at Tuskegee, beginning when it was a flight school for Black pilots who persevered despite the hostility of the surrounding White community: "Generation after generation, students here have shown that same grit, that same resilience to soar past obstacles and outrages, past the threat of countryside lynchings, past the humiliation of Jim Crow, past the turmoil of the Civil Rights era" (tuskegeevitrual, 2015). Noting that today's students may feel some pressure to live up to those who went before, she related her own experience facing the pressure of becoming the first African American first lady, as well as the racist micro- and macro-aggressions both she and her husband experienced on a regular basis:

> My husband and I know how frustrating that experience can be. We both felt the stings of those daily slights throughout our entire lives: the folks who crossed the streets in fear of their safety; the clerks who kept a close eye on us in all those department stores; the people at formal events who assumed we were the help—and those who have questioned our intelligence, our honesty, even our love of this country. (tuskegeevitrual, 2015)

In that speech, Obama also linked the injustices of the past to the present, noting that the indignities of racism, while a "heavy burden" that "can feel isolating," are "rooted in decades of structural challenges" that "are playing out in communities like Baltimore and Ferguson and so many others across this country" (tuskegeevitrual, 2015). However, she emphasized, they are not an excuse to give up or lose hope, or to give in to despair or anger. Rather, these frustrations should be channeled "into studies and organizing and banding together" to "build ourselves and our communities up" (tuskegeevitrual, 2015). The first step in this, she added, is to vote.

Motherhood and family

The second major theme in Obama's narrative is that family—and motherhood especially—are primary. Unlike the previous theme in which Obama explicitly linked her background to those of today's students in exhorting them to strive for the American Dream, the theme of motherhood and family was not presented as a goal for others. Rather, it was presented as her personal narrative, as that which is most dear to her heart—but also that to which other mothers could identify.

Obama frequently discussed her deep love for her daughters, as well as her conviction that raising them is her most important work. As she explained on the TV show *Entertainment Tonight*, "I've spent my children's entire life raising them to be independent, confident young women who are ready to build great lives for themselves" (Entertainment Tonight, 2015). In a variety of video clips and formats, she consistently makes it clear that, as she stated at the White House's Working Parents summit, "There is nothing more important to me than my girls" (The White House, 2014). Her primary concern, she added, is "making sure that my kids are whole." Indeed, during her speech at the 2012 Democratic National Convention, she emphasized that "at the end of the day, my most important title is still 'mom-in-chief.' My daughters are still the heart of my heart and the center of my world" (The New York Times, 2012). And in an interview on the *Today Show*, she stated, "I cherish my girls, and I'm so proud … so you know, they have my heart every single minute of every single day" (Today, 2015).

Obama also noted that placing her children as her first priority was not necessarily a popular decision. At the graduation ceremony at Tuskegee, after declaring that she is "first and foremost a mom," she added, "Look, I love our daughters more than anything in the world, more than life itself. And while that may not be the first thing that some folks want to hear from an Ivy League-educated lawyer, it is truly who I am. So for me, being mom in chief is, and always will be, job number one" (tuskegeevitrual, 2015).

Obama also characterized herself as a no-nonsense mother who does not coddle her children but wants them to understand how fortunate they are. In an interview with Barbara Walters, she explained, "We're always having that lesson—'You are blessed—you better understand this; I don't want to hear you complaining, because there are people with real issues'" (Townhall, 2012). Speaking at the Working Families summit, she stated that she and her husband want their girls to have the experience of working minimum wage jobs so that they will better understand what it is like for those who have "a job that's not fun" but, like her own father, do it to "put food on the table."

Obama's father, a Chicago water plant pump operator diagnosed with multiple sclerosis when she and her brother were young, was frequently mentioned as a source of love, motivation and inspiration. He worked every day, despite the pain, to provide for his family and to ensure that his children could have "the kind of education they could only dream of," she said at the 2012 Democratic National Conference.

In other YouTube clips, the first lady discussed attempts to normalize the White House for her daughters, the importance of family rituals, and how she and the president created opportunities to, as she stated in a *Today Show* clip, "just be a family" (Townhall, 2012). These include family dinners, when she and the president check in with their children about what is happening in their lives, and bedtime, when they tuck each other in. "We do a lot of tucking," she told Barbara Walters. "So the girls are like, 'I'm ready to be tucked! I'm ready to be tucked!' … So it's sort of our last, you know, check in" (Townhall, 2012). Obama also noted that she and the girls often dance together as a way to both have fun and get exercise. In addition, Obama said she invites all her cousins and relatives to the White House for Thanksgiving to replicate for her children the close community she had growing up with relatives nearby. And, like parents of any adolescent or teenager, she readily admitted that her children are often embarrassed by their parents—and that she and the president use the threat of public humiliation to keep them in line: "When you see us in a crowd, you'll find me whispering, 'Sit up straight, or I'm gonna embarrass you. I'm gonna start dancing.' And they're like, 'Mom, no, please don't!'" (Entertainment Tonight, 2015).

Obama also confided in a CNN interview that she worries about the effect on her children of raising them in the White House and works to keep them "sane" so "my girls come out of this on the other end whole" (CNN, 2012). In her Democratic National Convention speech, Obama similarly expressed early concerns about raising children in the White House as she outlined the lives she and her husband had created around them in Chicago:

> Our life before moving to Washington was filled with simple joys … Saturdays at soccer games, Sundays at grandma's house, and a date night for Barack and me was either dinner or a movie, because as an exhausted mom, I couldn't stay awake for both. And the truth is, I loved the life we had built for our girls. I deeply loved the man I had built that life with, and I didn't want that to change if he became president. (The New York Times, 2012)

The challenge of being a working mother prior to becoming first lady, of balancing work and family, was also central to this theme. For example, during the Working Families summit, Obama discussed the difficulties she faced as the wife of a state legislator and then a U.S. Senator who was frequently away from home while she was trying to hold down a part-time job and raise two young girls:

> We were still paying for full-time babysitting because as a professional, when there was a meeting that needed to happen, they expected you to be there. So we had to have full-time babysitting. So that was a net loss for us. Then I had Sasha and we lost our babysitter, which was probably the worst time of my motherhood. I was so devastated because that balance, that work–family balance is so fragile. And you realize how fragile it is that with a blink of an eye—of a broken toilet, a sick child, a sick parent—that that balance is thrown off. (The White House, 2014)

By foregrounding motherhood and family, this theme within Obama's narrative emphasizes a domesticity that appears universal, one to which mothers everywhere can relate. Anecdotes that highlight normal family rituals, her love for her daughters, her delight in their accomplishments, her desires for their success, and her acknowledgment of how they are embarrassed by her and their father, normalize Obama as a mother while, as Harris-Perry (2011) noted, rejecting the stereotype of the Mammy whose concern for White people supplants that for her own children.

Conclusion

The two primary themes found in this study—that through education, hard work, and perseverance, all is possible, and that motherhood and family are primary—are interwoven in Obama's narrative and attest to her having achieved the American Dream. For Obama, motherhood is very much a part of that dream—her most important work and accomplishment. In addition, in personal anecdotes and stories meant to inspire students to further their education, she is a role model in a narrative that is both motivational and inspirational: despite growing up in a working class family with limited financial resources, despite her Blackness, she has, through determination and effort, been rewarded—and so can others if they follow her example. The evidence of her success is an Ivy League education, a law degree, motherhood and family.

This narrative is, in essence, a neoliberal discourse, albeit with a twist that recognizes the structural inequalities of poverty and racism. Neoliberalism, "a mode of political and economic rationality characterized by privatization, deregulation and a rolling back and withdrawal of the state from many areas of social provision" (Gill & Scharff, 2011, p. 5), posits that success is a matter of choice, and if people make the right choices, free from the burdening oversight and control of government, they will be rewarded. Within neoliberalism, "all difference and the inequalities that result from them are seen as a matter of choice" (Ericson, Barry, & Doyle, 2000, p. 532). In its purest form, neoliberalism does not recognize systemic discrimination based on race, class, gender, sexuality, ability, or other aspects of socially constructed identity.

Although Obama's story acknowledges the challenges of racism and poverty, particularly in her Tuskegee speech, her recognition of gender bias is limited to the difficulties of raising children as a working mother, of balancing job demands with those of family, and the potential for disaster when a child is ill or the babysitter quits. Motherhood is the lens through which gendered inequities are viewed in this narrative: unequal pay, sexual harassment, gendered violence, and the myriad other forms of gendered discrimination and abuse in the workplace, home, and society are not included.

Indeed, even as Obama acknowledges the broad reach and impact of race and class oppressions, her unwavering assurance that the American Dream is within reach if only one tries hard enough, if only one has enough "grit," creates a narrative that fails to concede the intractability of the structural inequalities of class, race, and gender within a capitalist system in which the middle-class is shrinking, wages for working people have stagnated or lost ground, capital is increasingly concentrated in the hands of the upper 1%, upward mobility for successive generations is no longer assured (Piketty, 2014), educational opportunity is circumscribed by childhood poverty (Boland, 2016), and women and people of color are most harmed by the recent recession and global restructuring of the economy (Cooper, Gable, & Austin, 2012; Morrison, 2015). In addition, Obama's narrative adheres to the neoliberal notion of success measured through accomplishments that ultimately result in leaving the lower classes behind. A working-class job may be a respectable way-station, but one should not linger there.

All narratives are a construction, with some aspects highlighted whereas others are obscured or hidden. Public narratives such as Michelle Obama's are always constructed in ways that serve the interests of the teller. It is important to remember that in 2008, the public version of her story was composed by those who sought to portray her as a stereotypical angry, Black woman, and that even 4 years later, some YouTube videos portrayed Obama within the context of a new stereotype for accomplished African American women—the Powerful Black Bitch. It is against this backdrop of myths about and fear of Black women that the White House and Obama felt the need to reshape her narrative, to soften her image and rechoreograph her story. Harris-Perry (2011) claimed that the choices Obama made "to deflect, resist, redirect, or accommodate" public anxieties about her "Black womanhood" inevitably "suggest the limitations of individual strategies to challenge deeply embedded myths" (p. 277). The findings of this study attest to her argument. The decisions Michelle Obama and the White House made in telling her story—emphasizing the safely-gendered arena of family and motherhood, as well as the neoliberal ideology of individual responsibility and choice, with its concomitant emphasis on hard work, education and perseverance—were shaped and constrained by her race, class, and gender. Indeed, had Obama acknowledged the increasingly limited social mobility and greater income inequality in the United States (see, e.g., Piketty, 2014), as well as the role of a corporate elite in shaping U.S. laws and elections, she very likely would have fueled public fear and anger while being castigated once again as militant, unpatriotic and angry. Her public persona, the meta-image constructed for public consumption, was adapted to fit that which is socially acceptable within an environment only too willing to see her within the context of myths, fears and stereotypes about Black women.

Notes

1. In this and later references, Obama refers to the first lady, not her husband.
2. Although references to the White House normally refer to the president and his administrative staff, in the context of this study, it refers to both the president's West Wing staff as well as that of the first lady's staff in the East Wing of the White House.
3. See, for example, Gillborn (2015) and Moore (2012).
4. The Reach Higher initiative supports the president's "North Star" goal of re-achieving the U.S.'s former status as having the highest proportion of college graduates in the world.
5. For example, 85% of Columbia Height's Educational Campus' students qualify for free and reduced lunch; the Martin Luther King Jr. Magnet High School in Nashville has one of the city's most diverse student bodies, with almost 20% considered economically disadvantaged.

References

AussieNews1. (2014, February 6). *Michelle Obama 'I'm first' video* [Video File]. Retrieved from https://www.youtube.com/watch?v=r6plalYHuHc&list=PLaimFCPSKYmO1NxTvOEWsgJVYf1lt3Ym1&index=58

Boland, E. (2016). *The Battle for room 314: My year of hope and despair in a New York City high school.* New York, NY: Grand Central Publishing.

Brown, A. (2014, March 3). *Michelle Obama maintains positive image.* Retrieved from http://www.gallup.com/poll/167696/michelle-obama-maintains-positive-image.aspx?gsource=michelleobama

Cherlin, R. (2014). The worst wing: How the east wing shrank Michelle Obama. *New Republic.* Retrieved from https://newrepublic.com/article/117086/inside-east-wing-who-shrank-michelle-obama

Clark, C. (2012, August 13). Michelle Obama to serve as iVillage guest editor. *USA Today*. Retrieved from http://content.usatoday.com/communities/entertainment/post/2012/08/michelle-obama-to-serve-as-ivillage-guest-editor/1#.VzI7NhUrLp5

CNN. (2012, January 11). *Michelle Obama: I'm no angry black woman* [Video File]. Retrieved from https://www.youtube.com/watch?v=SbHa6vDwh6c&list=PLaimFCPSKYmO1NxTvOEWsgJVYf1lt3Ym1&index=30

CNN. (2013, June 5). *CNN exclusive: Michelle Obama confronts heckler* [Video File]. Retrieved from https://www.youtube.com/watch?v=aE09MScupks&list=PLaimFCPSKYmO1NxTvOEWsgJVYf1lt3Ym1&index=11

Collins, P. H. (2005). *Black sexual politics: African Americans, gender, and the new racism*. New York, NY: Routledge.

Cooper, D., Gable, M., & Austin, A. (2012). *The public-sector jobs crisis: Women and African Americans hit hardest by job losses in state and local governments*. Washington, DC: Economic Policy Institute.

Crenshaw, K. (1991). Mapping the margins: Intersectionality, identity, politics, and violence against women of colour. *Stanford Law Review*, *43*(6), 1241–1299.

Davis, A. Y. (1998). Women and capitalism: Dialectics of oppression and liberation. In J. James (Ed.), *The Angela Y. Davis reader* (pp. 161–192). Malden, MA: Blackwell.

Entertainment Tonight. (2015, May 1). *Michelle Obama on Sasha & Malia growing up: 'They're conditioning us for empty nest syndrome'* [Video File]. Retrieved from https://www.youtube.com/watch?v=w7PHgIod7jQ&list=PLaimFCPSKYmO1NxTvOEWsgJVYf1lt3Ym1&index=5

Ericson, R., Barry, D., & Doyle, A. (2000). The moral hazards of neo-liberalism: Lessons from the private insurance industry. *Economy and Society*, *29*, 532–558.

Gibbs, N., & Newton-Small, J. (2008). The war over Michelle Obama. *Time Magazine*. Retrieved from http://content.time.com/time/magazine/article/0,9171,1808642-1,00.html

Gill, R., & Scharff, C. (2011). *New femininities: Postfeminism, neoliberalism, and subjectivity*. New York, NY: Palgrave MacMillan.

Gillborn, D. (2015). Intersectionality, critical race theory, and the primacy of racism: Race, class, gender, and disability in education. *Qualitative Inquiry*, *21*, 277–287.

Glaser, B. S., & Strauss, A. (1967). *The discovery of grounded theory: Strategies for qualitative research*. Chicago, IL: Aldine.

Gopaldas, A. (2013). Intersectionality 101. *Journal of Public Policy & Marketing*, *32*, 90–94.

Harris-Perry, M. V. (2011). *Sister citizen: Shame, stereotypes, and Black women in America*. New Haven, CT: Yale University Press.

hooks, b. (1981). *Ain't I a woman: Black women and feminism*. Boston, MA: South End Press.

iVillage. (2012, August 24). *Michelle Obama on her female friendships: "My saviors"* [Video File]. Retrieved from https://www.youtube.com/watch?v=5DChnZzdiUM&list=PLaimFCPSKYmO1NxTvOEWsgJVYf1lt3Ym1&index=48

Leitch, T. M. (1986). *What stories are: Narrative theory and interpretation*. University Park, PA: Pennsylvania State University Press.

Lieblich, A., Tuval-Mashiach, R., & Zilber, T. (1998). *Narrative research: Reading, analysis, and interpretation*. Thousand Oaks, CA: Sage.

Lugo-Lugo, C. R., & Bloodsworth-Lugo, M. K. (2011). Bare biceps and American (in)security: Post-9/11 constructions of safe(ty), threat, and the first Black first lady. *WSQ: Women's Studies Quarterly*, *39*(1), 200–217.

McIntee, M. (2015, June 11). *Michelle Obama on race & success at Chicago hs graduation* [Video File]. Retrieved from https://www.youtube.com/watch?v=imXogqDPYk c&list=PLaimFCPSKYmO1NxTvOEWsgJVYf1lt3Ym1&index=19

Meyers, M. (2013). *African American women in the news: Gender, race, and class in journalism*. New York, NY: Routledge.

Moore, M. (2012). Intersectionality and the study of Black, sexual minority women. *Gender & Society, 26*(1), 33–39.

Morrison, A. (2015). Black unemployment rate 2015: In better economy, African-Americans see minimal gains. *International Business Times*. Retrieved from http://www.ibtimes.com/black-unemployment-rate-2015-better-economy-african-americans-see-minimal-gains-1837870

Mortensen, T. (2015). Visually assessing the First Lady in a digital age: A study of Michelle Obama as portrayed by journalists and the White House. *Journal of Women, Politics & Policy, 36*(1), 43–67.

Palser, B. (2006). Missed opportunities: News sites should make better use of the material provided by YouTube and other Internet resources. *American Journalism Review, 28*(4), 84–85.

Pickler, N. (2008, June 13). Fighting slurs, lies and videotape. *Toronto Star*, p. A2.

Piketty, T. (2014). *Capital in the twenty-first century*. Cambridge, MA: Harvard University Press.

Reeves, J. L., & Campbell, R. (1994). *Cracked coverage: Television news, the anti-cocaine crusade, and the Reagan legacy*. Durham, NC: Duke University Press.

Riessman, C. K. (1993). *Narrative analysis*. Newbury Park, CA: Sage.

Shoop, T. J. (2010). From professionals to potential First Ladies: How newspapers told the stories of Cindy McCain and Michelle Obama. *Sex Roles, 63*, 807–819.

Smith, J. (2015). The upside of "uppity": Turning a racial slur into a symbol of power and steadfastness. *The New Republic*, 10–11.

Spillers, H. (2009). Views of the East Wing: On Michelle Obama. *Communication and Critical/Cultural Studies, 6*, 307–310.

Steyn, M. (2008). Mrs. Obama's America. *National Review*. Retrieved from http://www.freerepublic.com/focus/f-news/2006753/posts

Strangelove, M. (2010). *Watching YouTube: Extraordinary videos by ordinary people*. Toronto, Canada: University of Toronto Press.

The Book Archive. (2013, December 9). *Michelle Obama on the importance of higher education: College students speech* [Video File]. Retrieved from https://www.youtube.com/watch?V=KS8COqXsZvg&list=PLyKic_f7lZkb-UEYgDwN8SBAk0C3xScAz&index=19

The New York Times. (2012, September 4). *Election 2012: Michelle Obama's DNC speech* [Video File]. Retrieved from https://www.youtube.com/watch?v=cvZ5nPFW5H8&index=13&list=PLaimFCPSKYmO1NxTvOEWsgJVYf1lt3Ym

The White House. (2013, April 10). *First Lady Michelle Obama speaks at meeting to address youth violence* [Video File]. Retrieved from https://www.youtube.com/watch?v=yY46XyhXiq0&index=19&list=PLaimFCPSKYmO1NxTvOEWsgJVYf1lt3Ym

The White House. (2014, June 23). *The first lady speaks at the working families summit* [Video File]. Retrieved from https://www.youtube.com/watch?v=N7Biilj2XIg&index=54&list=PLaimFCPSKYmO1NxTvOEWsgJVYf1lt3Ym1

The White House. (2015, July 23). *The first lady hosts the "beating the odds" summit* [Video File]. Retrieved from https://www.youtube.com/watch?v=6Sv90RgTSws&list=PLaimFCPSKYmO1NxTvOEWsgJVYf1lt3Ym1&index=9

Today. (2015, February 11). *Michelle Obama's modern re-design of the White House* [Video File]. Retrieved from https://www.youtube.com/watch?v=xbV1GwI07O4&index=4&list=PLaimFCPSKYmO1NxTvOEWsgJVYf1lt3Ym1

Townhall. (2012, September 25). *Barack & Michelle Obama on the "View" [Complete]* [Video File]. Retrieved from https://www.youtube.com/watch?v=Hdn1iX1a528&list=PLaimFCPSKYmO1NxTvOEWsgJVYf1lt3Ym1&index=5

tuskegeevirtual. (2015, May 11). *Michelle Obama's full speech at Tuskegee University* [Video File]. Retrieved from https://www.youtube.com/watch?v=qhUKwl5NFgE

Index

Note: Tables are indicated by **bold**. Endnotes are indicated by the page number followed by 'n' and the endnote number e.g., 20n1 refers to endnote 1 on page 20.

Adams, A. 2
affordable care act 4, 14
Althusser, L. 3, 21, 23, 32
analysis of variance (ANOVA) analysis 81
anti-black affect 3, 52, 57, 60, 63, 65, 66

Barrett, T. 26
Beasley, V. B. 97
Berger, J. 33
Bergsieker, H. B. 55
black anger modeled, James Baldwin: contextualization 38; democratic faith 48; joy/pain 37; juxtaposition 38; Obama and his critics 41–2; outrage/political lynchings 39–41; race 44–5; racial inequality 39; rhetoric/anger/ hope 45–8; violence/rhetoric/ civic polity 42–4; white supremacy 38
black feminist theories 110
black leader 2
black masculinity 2; challenges 8–9; clarification humor 13–14; comedic presence 7; emancipatory model 7; hallmark characteristics 7; impassioned feelings 6; Kenyan Muslim, comic lens of enforcement 10–12; Obama's humor/rhetorical effect 9–10; Obama's racio-rhetorical style 14–17; political legacy 17–18
Bloodsworth-Lugo, M. K. 109
Bourdieu, P. 23
Boys, S. 2
Bromell, N. 39
Brown Givens, S. M. 53
Brown, A. 107
Brown, C. 2
Brown, S. H. 42

caricature 70; angry black woman 72; anti-/ un-American 87; cultural hybridity 71; hypothetical young white republican **84**; iconographical analysis **78**; iconographical/ survey data analyses 71, 85; iconography 74–5; multimethod approach 75–7; multinomial logistic regression **82**; news attentiveness model predicting response **82**; public attitudes 81–4; race/party identification **81**; results 78–81; skepticism 72; visual communication 71, 84, 86; visual communication, New Yorker 72–4
Cherlin, R. 108
Coates, T. 1
Cogburn, D. 2
congressional cooperative election study (CCES) 76
Cooper, R. 1
constant comparative method 112
Couldry, N. 22
counter-stereotypical exemplars 54, 56, 63

Dyson, M. 1

Engels, J. 42
Espinoza-Vasque, F. 2

Fiske, S. T. 55, 56
Frank, D. A. 42
Franklin, C. W. 17

glass cliff effect 57, 64
Glastris, P. 1
Glaude, E. S. 41
Gleason, T. R. 20, 21, 27
Glenn, R. E. 4, 91
Goman, C. 106
Greenfield, J. 48n2

hall's reception analysis 27
Hall, S. 26, 27, 29
Hansen, S. S. 20
Hariman, R. 26, 27
Harris-Perry, M. V. 119
health care reform 1
hegemonic position 26
Hope, D. S. 26
Hu, S. 1

iconographical symbolism 75
ideological state apparatus (ISA) 21

image control: Althusser's ISA 22–4; conflict 31–2; exploratory research questions 24; image descriptions, White House flickr URLs **25**; impression management 21; ISA 21; meeting room settings, leadership, 29–30; method 25; modern political image management 20; neutral spaces to share power 31; photojournalism routine 21–2; photojournalists 34; press-excluded events 27; press-excluded photos 26–7; routine practices of the press 32–3; social brand building 21; traditional images, American symbolism 33–4; visual rhetoric 25–6; visual rhetoric analysis 21; White House photos, symbols/meanings, 28–9
Indian Healthcare Improvement Act 4, 102
Isaksen, J. L. 6, 38

King-Meadows T. D. 70
Kurtz , J. B. 4, 37

Logan, E. L. 51–53
Lucaites, J. L. 26, 27
Lugo-Lugo, C. R. 109

Martinez, A. R. 51
McCorkindale, T. 2
McCue-Enser, M. 2
Mercieca, J. R. 57
Meyer, J. C. 10, 11, 13
Meyers, M. 106, 110, 111
Meyers, S. 7
Mortensen, T. 3, 107, 109

nation-state, tribal nations: adoption 99, 98; American identity construction 98; decolonizing strategy 100; government-to-government 97; indigenous communities 96; indigenous leaders 99; indigenous tribes 97, 99; nation-to-nation relationships 99; redskins 101; tribal sovereignty 96
neoliberal narrative: black feminist 110; black women 119; constructing narrative 112; education, hard work/perseverance/American dream 113–15; gender inequities 108; intersectionality 110; literature review 108–10; motherhood/family 115–17; narrative analysis 111; negative public perceptions 107; neoliberal discourse 118; neoliberal ideology 108; new republic 106; race/class oppressions 118; traditional media 108; video press releases 111; White House 110, 111, 120n2
Nosek, B. A. 53, 55

Obama Don't Care 14, 15
Obama's baby mama 106
Obama's Racio-rhetorical humor *see* Black masculinity
Olson, L. C. 26

Panofsky's iconographical framework 74
politics of fear *see* caricature
political lynchings 40, 48n2
postracial contemporary American society 52

racialized news framing/symbolic racism: American dream 53–4; aversive racism 64; Black leaders 66; counter-stereotypic exemplars 52, 63; counter-stereotypical exemplar 54–6; dependent variables 60–1; enlightened racism 64; heuristic effects 67; media celebrities 52–3; media coverage 51; method 58; multiculturalism 52; results 61–3; scrutiny/tokenism/presidential burdens 56–7; symbolic racist beliefs 52; Whites' racial attitudes 66
racialized scrutiny 56
Ramasubramanian, S. 51
repressive state apparatus (RSA) 22
Riessman, C. K. 111
Rossing, J. P. 11
Russell, A. M. 55

Schmidt, K. 53, 55
Seinfeld, J. 6, 7
Shaw, M. E. 8
Smith, J. 107
Stevens, E. M. 70
symbolic racism 60–1
Sweet, D. 2

Terrill, R. E. 41
Thomson, M. 24
tribal nations conferences 4; Cherokee referendum 92; indigenous sovereign nations 93–6; limit tribal membership 91; nation-state 96–7; sovereign/nation 93; state of nations 103; systemic racial discrimination 103; watershed moment 92
Turner, J. 38

Vaughn, J. S. 57
visual rhetoric's qualitative methodology 26

Waisanen, D. 9
Waldman, P. 1, 4
wall street reform 1
Watson, E. 8
West, C. 1
White House Correspondents Dinner (WHCD) 11
White House events 3
White House's photographs 26
white racial frame 73
white supremacy 38
Williams, E. W. 17
Williams, L. 55
Wilmore, L. 10, 14–18
Wingfield, A. H. 56
Wingfield, J. H. 56